JAMESTOWN EDUCATION

Reading Fluency

Reader's Record

Level
C

Camille L. Z. Blachowicz, Ph.D.

JAMESTOWN ☙ EDUCATION

Reading Fluency

Reader's Record

Level C

Camille L. Z. Blachowicz, Ph.D.

McGraw Hill **Glencoe**

New York, New York   Columbus, Ohio   Chicago, Illinois   Peoria, Illinois   Woodland Hills, California

JAMESTOWN  EDUCATION

Mc Graw Hill **Glencoe**

The *McGraw·Hill* Companies

Send all inquiries to:
Glencoe/McGraw-Hill
8787 Orion Place
Columbus, OH 43240-4027

ISBN 0-07-845700-9
Printed in the United States of America.
3 4 5 6 7 8 9 10 021 09 08 07

Contents

How to Use These Books

The Reading Fluency *Reader* contains 72 reading passages. The accompanying *Reader's Record* contains two copies of each of these passages and includes a place for marking *miscues*. You and your partner will take turns using the *Reader*. Each of you will need your own *Reader's Record*. You will also need a stopwatch or a timer.

What Are Miscues?

Miscues are errors or slips that all readers make. These include the following:
- a mispronounced word
- a word substituted for the correct word
- an inserted word
- a skipped word

Repeating a word or correcting oneself immediately is not counted as a miscue.

What Procedure Do I Follow?

1. Work with a partner. One partner is the reader; the other partner is the recorder.

2. Suppose that you are the first to read aloud. Read a selection from the *Reader* as your partner marks any miscues you make on the corresponding page in your *Reader's Record*. The recorder's job is to listen carefully and make a tick mark above each place in the text where a miscue occurs, and to make a slash mark indicating where you stop reading after "Time!" is called.

3. The recorder says when to start and calls "Time!" after a minute.

4. After the reading, the recorder:
   - counts the number of words read, using the number guides at the right-hand side of the passage, and records the Total Words Read
   - writes the total number of miscues for each line in the far right-hand column labeled Miscues. Totals and records the miscues on the Total Errors line
   - subtracts Total Errors from Total Words Read to find the Correct Words Per Minute (WPM) and records that score on the Correct WPM line

5. You review the *Reader's Record*, noting your miscues. Discuss with your partner the characteristics of good reading you have displayed. Then rate your own performance and mark the scale at the bottom of the page.

6. Change roles with your partner and repeat the procedure.

7. You and your partner then begin a second round of reading the same passage. When it is your turn to read, try to improve in pace, expression, and accuracy over the first reading.

8. After completing two readings, record your Correct WPM scores in the back of your *Reader's Record*. Follow the directions on the graph.

1

Fiction

from *Coast to Coast*
by Betsy Byars

First Reading

	Words Read	Miscues

"Birch, the airplane is sold."   5   _____

"You haven't got the money yet."   11   _____

"I don't want to take any chances."   18   _____

"See? Don't take any chances—that's exactly what getting old   28   _____
is. Don't step on the grass. Don't go out of the yard!"   40   _____

"That's enough. I mean it."   45   _____

Birch was silent for a moment. Then in a different voice, as if   58   _____
she were taking up a new topic, she said, "You never have taken   71   _____
me up."   73   _____

Her grandfather glanced at the sky. Beneath her eyeshade,   82   _____
Birch's eyes narrowed. She knew she had him now.   91   _____

"I really want to go!" As she said it, she realized it was true.   105   _____
She needed to get away from this world, and this was the way to   119   _____
do it. "What are we waiting for?"   126   _____

"I don't guess it would hurt to fly to the beach and back."   139   _____

"Then get in! Let's go!"   144   _____

"Don't get in too big a hurry." Her grandfather smiled. It was   156   _____
his first real smile of the afternoon.   163   _____

Birch followed him around the plane. "What are you doing?"   173   _____

"Well, right now, I'm doing a preflight inspection. I check the   184   _____
tires, the control surfaces, move them for freedom and cable   194   _____
looseness."   195   _____

Needs Work   1   2   3   4   5   Excellent
Paid attention to punctuation

Needs Work   1   2   3   4   5   Excellent
Sounded good

Total Words Read _____

Total Errors − _____

Correct WPM _____

from *Coast to Coast*

by Betsy Byars

	Words Read	Miscues
"Birch, the airplane is sold."	5	_____
"You haven't got the money yet."	11	_____
"I don't want to take any chances."	18	_____
"See? Don't take any chances—that's exactly what getting old	28	_____
is. Don't step on the grass. Don't go out of the yard!"	40	_____
"That's enough. I mean it."	45	_____
Birch was silent for a moment. Then in a different voice, as if	58	_____
she were taking up a new topic, she said, "You never have taken	71	_____
me up."	73	_____
Her grandfather glanced at the sky. Beneath her eyeshade,	82	_____
Birch's eyes narrowed. She knew she had him now.	91	_____
"I really want to go!" As she said it, she realized it was true.	105	_____
She needed to get away from this world, and this was the way to	119	_____
do it. "What are we waiting for?"	126	_____
"I don't guess it would hurt to fly to the beach and back."	139	_____
"Then get in! Let's go!"	144	_____
"Don't get in too big a hurry." Her grandfather smiled. It was	156	_____
his first real smile of the afternoon.	163	_____
Birch followed him around the plane. "What are you doing?"	173	_____
"Well, right now, I'm doing a preflight inspection. I check the	184	_____
tires, the control surfaces, move them for freedom and cable	194	_____
looseness."	195	_____

Needs Work   1   2   3   4   5   Excellent
Paid attention to punctuation

Needs Work   1   2   3   4   5   Excellent
Sounded good

Total Words Read _____

Total Errors − _____

Correct WPM _____

2

2
Fiction

from *My Side of the Mountain*

by Jean Craighead George

First Reading

	Words Read	Miscues

"Well, Baron Weasel!" I said in astonishment. I was sure it was | 12 | _____

the same weasel I had met in the trap. He was on the boulder in | 27 | _____

front of the hemlock, batting the ferns with his front feet and | 39 | _____

rearing and staring at me. | 44 | _____

"Now, you stay right there," I said. Of course, he flipped and | 56 | _____

came off the rock like a jet stream. He was at the door before I | 71 | _____

could stop him, loping around my feet like a bouncing ball. | 82 | _____

"You look glad all over, Baron. I hope all that frisking means | 94 | _____

joy," I said. He took my pants leg in his teeth, tugged it, and then | 109 | _____

rippled softly back to the boulder. He went down a small hole. | 121 | _____

He popped up again, bit a fern near by, and ran around the | 134 | _____

boulder. I crept out to look for him—no weasel. I poked a stick | 148 | _____

in the hole at the base of the rock trying to provoke him. I felt a | 164 | _____

little jumpy, so that when a shot rang out through the woods I | 177 | _____

leapt a foot in the air. . . . A cricket chirped, a catbird scratched | 189 | _____

the leaves. I waited. One enormous minute later a dark form ran | 201 | _____

onto the meadow. It stumbled and fell. | 208 | _____

Needs Work 1 2 3 4 5 Excellent
Paid attention to punctuation

Needs Work 1 2 3 4 5 Excellent
Sounded good

Total Words Read _____

Total Errors − _____

Correct WPM _____

2

Fiction

from *My Side of the Mountain*
by Jean Craighead George

	Words Read	Miscues

"Well, Baron Weasel!" I said in astonishment. I was sure it was   12 _____

the same weasel I had met in the trap. He was on the boulder in   27 _____

front of the hemlock, batting the ferns with his front feet and   39 _____

rearing and staring at me.   44 _____

"Now, you stay right there," I said. Of course, he flipped and   56 _____

came off the rock like a jet stream. He was at the door before I   71 _____

could stop him, loping around my feet like a bouncing ball.   82 _____

"You look glad all over, Baron. I hope all that frisking means   94 _____

joy," I said. He took my pants leg in his teeth, tugged it, and then   109 _____

rippled softly back to the boulder. He went down a small hole.   121 _____

He popped up again, bit a fern near by, and ran around the   134 _____

boulder. I crept out to look for him—no weasel. I poked a stick   148 _____

in the hole at the base of the rock trying to provoke him. I felt a   164 _____

little jumpy, so that when a shot rang out through the woods I   177 _____

leapt a foot in the air. . . . A cricket chirped, a catbird scratched   189 _____

the leaves. I waited. One enormous minute later a dark form ran   201 _____

onto the meadow. It stumbled and fell.   208 _____

Needs Work   1 2 3 4 5   Excellent
Paid attention to punctuation

Needs Work   1 2 3 4 5   Excellent
Sounded good

Total Words Read   _____

Total Errors − _____

Correct WPM   _____

3

Fiction

from "The Professor of Smells"
by Laurence Yep

⚬⚬⚬⚬

First Reading

	Words Read	Miscues

"Professor Chung," the official announced solemnly, "word has **8** _____

reached His Imperial Highness of your special skills. He begs **18** _____

you to come to the capital right away. His jade seal has been lost. **32** _____

No document is official without it. The government is paralyzed. **42** _____

An army of soldiers and clerks has searched the palace; but **53** _____

they could find nothing now. Your country turns to you now in **65** _____

its hour of need. You must find the lost seal." **75** _____

Chung, the gambler thought to himself, you're in for it now. **86** _____

And out loud he said, "It's impossible. I have no such talents." **98** _____

"This is no time to be modest," his wife hissed at him. **110** _____

The official tapped him with his fan. "Your wife is right. Anyway, **122** _____

you have no choice. His Imperial Highness summons you." **131** _____

Chung clutched at his head and bowed. "You have to believe **142** _____

me. I'm telling the truth. I'm a fraud." **150** _____

But the official signed to some soldiers. . . . **157** _____

All the way to the palace, Chung imagined what would happen. **168** _____

"Chung," he said to himself, "it's only fair if they torture you. You've **181** _____

been a cheat and a liar all your life. But then they'll punish your **195** _____

wife and all your kin and all your neighbors, and that isn't fair." **208** _____

By the time they had reached the audience hall, he had scared **220** _____

himself thoroughly. **222** _____

Needs Work   1   2   3   4   5   Excellent
Paid attention to punctuation

Needs Work   1   2   3   4   5   Excellent
Sounded good

Total Words Read _____

Total Errors − _____

Correct WPM _____

3

Fiction

from "The Professor of Smells"
by Laurence Yep

	Words Read	Miscues

"Professor Chung," the official announced solemnly, "word has ⟶ 8 _____

reached His Imperial Highness of your special skills. He begs ⟶ 18 _____

you to come to the capital right away. His jade seal has been lost. ⟶ 32 _____

No document is official without it. The government is paralyzed. ⟶ 42 _____

An army of soldiers and clerks has searched the palace; but ⟶ 53 _____

they could find nothing now. Your country turns to you now in ⟶ 65 _____

its hour of need. You must find the lost seal." ⟶ 75 _____

Chung, the gambler thought to himself, you're in for it now. ⟶ 86 _____

And out loud he said, "It's impossible. I have no such talents." ⟶ 98 _____

"This is no time to be modest," his wife hissed at him. ⟶ 110 _____

The official tapped him with his fan. "Your wife is right. Anyway, ⟶ 122 _____

you have no choice. His Imperial Highness summons you." ⟶ 131 _____

Chung clutched at his head and bowed. "You have to believe ⟶ 142 _____

me. I'm telling the truth. I'm a fraud." ⟶ 150 _____

But the official signed to some soldiers. . . . ⟶ 157 _____

All the way to the palace, Chung imagined what would happen. ⟶ 168 _____

"Chung," he said to himself, "it's only fair if they torture you. You've ⟶ 181 _____

been a cheat and a liar all your life. But then they'll punish your ⟶ 195 _____

wife and all your kin and all your neighbors, and that isn't fair." ⟶ 208 _____

By the time they had reached the audience hall, he had scared ⟶ 220 _____

himself thoroughly. ⟶ 222 _____

Needs Work   1   2   3   4   5   Excellent
         Paid attention to punctuation

Needs Work   1   2   3   4   5   Excellent
              Sounded good

Total Words Read   _____

Total Errors   − _____

Correct WPM   _____

4
Fiction

from *Red Cap*
by G. Clifton Wisler

First Reading

	Words Read	Miscues

[It] was May when Captain Jayroe visited Frostburg. He   9   _____
brought along a wagon and was signing up farmboys and miners   20   _____
for a new regiment of loyal Virginians.   27   _____

"Tenth Regiment, Virginia Unionists, we're to be called," he   36   _____
told me when I helped him water his horse outside the forge.   48   _____
"My company forms at Piedmont, Virginia."   54   _____

"My name's Ransom J. Powell," I told him. "I've been looking   65   _____
to join up myself."   69   _____

"You?" he asked with raised eyebrows. "How old are you?"   79   _____

"Fifteen," I lied. . . .   82   _____

"Can you beat a drum?" he asked.   89   _____

I dashed into the barn and produced my sticks. In short order   101   _____
I tapped a tune or two on my knee.   110   _____

"Not bad," he said, scowling. "But fifteen?"   117   _____

"I run smallish," I argued.   122   _____

"You'd be smallish at twelve, Powell. But as it happens, we'll   133   _____
need a boy to beat the drum. . . .   140   _____

"Talk it over with your family then. And if they're agreeable to   152   _____
the notion, join us in Piedmont. You understand?"   160   _____

"Yes, sir," I assured him.   165   _____

I didn't talk over anything with Pa. Nor Ma, either, knowing   176   _____
their views. I wrote them a letter with my goodbyes in it, and I   190   _____
tucked it under Ma's teakettle in the kitchen.   198   _____

Needs Work   1   2   3   4   5   Excellent
Paid attention to punctuation

Needs Work   1   2   3   4   5   Excellent
Sounded good

Total Words Read _____

Total Errors − _____

Correct WPM _____

from *Red Cap*

by G. Clifton Wisler

[It] was May when Captain Jayroe visited Frostburg. He	9	_____
brought along a wagon and was signing up farmboys and miners	20	_____
for a new regiment of loyal Virginians.	27	_____
"Tenth Regiment, Virginia Unionists, we're to be called," he	36	_____
told me when I helped him water his horse outside the forge.	48	_____
"My company forms at Piedmont, Virginia."	54	_____
"My name's Ransom J. Powell," I told him. "I've been looking	65	_____
to join up myself."	69	_____
"You?" he asked with raised eyebrows. "How old are you?"	79	_____
"Fifteen," I lied. . . .	82	_____
"Can you beat a drum?" he asked.	89	_____
I dashed into the barn and produced my sticks. In short order	101	_____
I tapped a tune or two on my knee.	110	_____
"Not bad," he said, scowling. "But fifteen?"	117	_____
"I run smallish," I argued.	122	_____
"You'd be smallish at twelve, Powell. But as it happens, we'll	133	_____
need a boy to beat the drum. . . .	140	_____
"Talk it over with your family then. And if they're agreeable to	152	_____
the notion, join us in Piedmont. You understand?"	160	_____
"Yes, sir," I assured him.	165	_____
I didn't talk over anything with Pa. Nor Ma, either, knowing	176	_____
their views. I wrote them a letter with my goodbyes in it, and I	190	_____
tucked it under Ma's teakettle in the kitchen.	198	_____

Needs Work   1   2   3   4   5   Excellent
Paid attention to punctuation

Needs Work   1   2   3   4   5   Excellent
Sounded good

Total Words Read _____

Total Errors − _____

Correct WPM _____

5

Fiction

from *Santiago's Silver Mine*
by Eleanor Clymer

First Reading

	Words Read	Miscues

She began to tell us another story. It was about a man who was | 14 | _____

so poor that he had nothing to eat, and his children were crying | 27 | _____

with hunger. His wife told him to go out and find something. So | 40 | _____

he went out and wandered around in the night, till he came to a | 54 | _____

mountain. He started to climb up the mountain, thinking, "It is | 65 | _____

no use. I might as well climb up and sit on the top of this | 80 | _____

mountain till I die." | 84 | _____

But halfway up he came to an opening in the mountain. The | 96 | _____

doors were wide open, and it was brightly lighted inside. He went | 108 | _____

in and saw many people. There were piles of delicious foods, just | 120 | _____

like a market. A man came over and said to him, "Take some, | 133 | _____

take some." | 135 | _____

He said, "But I have no money." | 142 | _____

The man said, "It doesn't matter, take whatever you like. But I | 154 | _____

must warn you, at twelve o'clock the doors will close, and you will | 167 | _____

have to stay here all night. So hurry up." | 176 | _____

So the poor man took a few handfuls of beans and mangoes | 188 | _____

and some chili peppers and corn, and hurried out. | 197 | _____

Needs Work   1   2   3   4   5   Excellent
Paid attention to punctuation

Needs Work   1   2   3   4   5   Excellent
Sounded good

Total Words Read _____

Total Errors − _____

Correct WPM _____

from *Santiago's Silver Mine*
by Eleanor Clymer

	Words Read	Miscues

She began to tell us another story. It was about a man who was — 14 _____

so poor that he had nothing to eat, and his children were crying — 27 _____

with hunger. His wife told him to go out and find something. So — 40 _____

he went out and wandered around in the night, till he came to a — 54 _____

mountain. He started to climb up the mountain, thinking, "It is — 65 _____

no use. I might as well climb up and sit on the top of this — 80 _____

mountain till I die." — 84 _____

But halfway up he came to an opening in the mountain. The — 96 _____

doors were wide open, and it was brightly lighted inside. He went — 108 _____

in and saw many people. There were piles of delicious foods, just — 120 _____

like a market. A man came over and said to him, "Take some, — 133 _____

take some." — 135 _____

He said, "But I have no money." — 142 _____

The man said, "It doesn't matter, take whatever you like. But I — 154 _____

must warn you, at twelve o'clock the doors will close, and you will — 167 _____

have to stay here all night. So hurry up." — 176 _____

So the poor man took a few handfuls of beans and mangoes — 188 _____

and some chili peppers and corn, and hurried out. — 197 _____

Needs Work 1 2 3 4 5 Excellent
Paid attention to punctuation

Needs Work 1 2 3 4 5 Excellent
Sounded good

Total Words Read _____

Total Errors − _____

Correct WPM _____

6 Nonfiction

from *Sacagawea: Indian Guide*
by Wyatt Blassingame

First Reading

	Words Read	Miscues

It was September, but in the high mountains snow had begun   11   _____
to fall. All the game was gone. The men ate any berries they could   25   _____
find, and the roots Sacagawea dug. Once a starving wolf came   36   _____
close to the camp. The men killed and ate it.   46   _____

Sacagawea remembered how her people had lived. They always   55   _____
had to leave the mountains in winter or starve. But these white   67   _____
men kept going west, deeper into the mountains.   75   _____

Captain Clark hurt his hip and could hardly walk. Captain   85   _____
Lewis was sick. Most of the men were sick or hurt. All were weak   99   _____
from hunger. One day there was nothing to eat but a few candles.   112   _____
Silently Sacagawea ate the small piece given to her. She knew she   124   _____
must save all the strength possible. She had to nurse [her son]   136   _____
Little Pomp.   138   _____

At last the terrible trail began to go down hill. They came to   151   _____
a valley filled with green grass. They had crossed the Rocky   162   _____
Mountains!   163   _____

Here was a river with many fish in it. Sacagawea and the men   176   _____
ate fish until they were filled. Then the men cut down trees and   189   _____
built boats. From here they could float downstream.   197   _____

All the way up the Missouri River they had seen few Indians.   209   _____
Now they passed village after village, first on the Snake River,   220   _____
then on the Columbia.   224   _____

Needs Work   1   2   3   4   5   Excellent
Paid attention to punctuation

Needs Work   1   2   3   4   5   Excellent
Sounded good

Total Words Read   _____

Total Errors − _____

Correct WPM   _____

6

Nonfiction

from *Sacagawea: Indian Guide*
by Wyatt Blassingame

	Words Read	Miscues
It was September, but in the high mountains snow had begun	11	_____
to fall. All the game was gone. The men ate any berries they could	25	_____
find, and the roots Sacagawea dug. Once a starving wolf came	36	_____
close to the camp. The men killed and ate it.	46	_____
Sacagawea remembered how her people had lived. They always	55	_____
had to leave the mountains in winter or starve. But these white	67	_____
men kept going west, deeper into the mountains.	75	_____
Captain Clark hurt his hip and could hardly walk. Captain	85	_____
Lewis was sick. Most of the men were sick or hurt. All were weak	99	_____
from hunger. One day there was nothing to eat but a few candles.	112	_____
Silently Sacagawea ate the small piece given to her. She knew she	124	_____
must save all the strength possible. She had to nurse [her son]	136	_____
Little Pomp.	138	_____
At last the terrible trail began to go down hill. They came to	151	_____
a valley filled with green grass. They had crossed the Rocky	162	_____
Mountains!	163	_____
Here was a river with many fish in it. Sacagawea and the men	176	_____
ate fish until they were filled. Then the men cut down trees and	189	_____
built boats. From here they could float downstream.	197	_____
All the way up the Missouri River they had seen few Indians.	209	_____
Now they passed village after village, first on the Snake River,	220	_____
then on the Columbia.	224	_____

Needs Work 1 2 3 4 5 Excellent
Paid attention to punctuation

Needs Work 1 2 3 4 5 Excellent
Sounded good

Total Words Read _____

Total Errors − _____

Correct WPM _____

7

Nonfiction

from *Stars Come Out Within*
by Jean Little

	Words Read	Miscues

"All right, Miss Little. Your turn next," Doug Roberts said.   10 _____

He sounded as though he was positive that [the seeing-eye   20 _____

dog] Zephyr and I would do beautifully. I gulped and clambered   31 _____

awkwardly out onto the walk. We were on a quiet side street that   44 _____

cut across Maple Avenue.   48 _____

"Bring him alongside of you. That's it. Relax, Miss Little."   58 _____

He checked to see that I was holding the leash threaded through   70 _____

my fingers properly and that my hand was curled around but not   82 _____

clutching the handle. I had it right. I felt very slightly smug.   94 _____

"Fine. Now go straight ahead to the corner," Mr. Roberts said   105 _____

as he fell back a pace.   111 _____

I took a shaking breath and cleared my throat.   120 _____

"Zephyr, forward," I said. The husky voice speaking those   129 _____

words sounded like a stranger's.   134 _____

Then Zephyr obeyed. Without stopping to stare up at me, he   145 _____

went calmly and competently ahead and, tugging me after him,   155 _____

led the way to the corner. When he reached the curb, he stopped.   168 _____

So did I. He glanced up at me inquiringly. He was actually waiting   181 _____

for me to tell him what to do next. He believed in me.   194 _____

"Cross here and, when you get to the corner opposite, turn   205 _____

right," Mr. Roberts told me. "And don't forget to praise him."   216 _____

"Good boy, Zephyr," I said hastily.   222 _____

Needs Work   1 2 3 4 5   Excellent
_____
Paid attention to punctuation

Needs Work   1 2 3 4 5   Excellent
_____
Sounded good

Total Words Read _____

Total Errors − _____

Correct WPM _____

from *Stars Come Out Within*

by Jean Little

	Words Read	Miscues
"All right, Miss Little. Your turn next," Doug Roberts said.	10	_____
He sounded as though he was positive that [the seeing-eye	20	_____
dog] Zephyr and I would do beautifully. I gulped and clambered	31	_____
awkwardly out onto the walk. We were on a quiet side street that	44	_____
cut across Maple Avenue.	48	_____
"Bring him alongside of you. That's it. Relax, Miss Little."	58	_____
He checked to see that I was holding the leash threaded through	70	_____
my fingers properly and that my hand was curled around but not	82	_____
clutching the handle. I had it right. I felt very slightly smug.	94	_____
"Fine. Now go straight ahead to the corner," Mr. Roberts said	105	_____
as he fell back a pace.	111	_____
I took a shaking breath and cleared my throat.	120	_____
"Zephyr, forward," I said. The husky voice speaking those	129	_____
words sounded like a stranger's.	134	_____
Then Zephyr obeyed. Without stopping to stare up at me, he	145	_____
went calmly and competently ahead and, tugging me after him,	155	_____
led the way to the corner. When he reached the curb, he stopped.	168	_____
So did I. He glanced up at me inquiringly. He was actually waiting	181	_____
for me to tell him what to do next. He believed in me.	194	_____
"Cross here and, when you get to the corner opposite, turn	205	_____
right," Mr. Roberts told me. "And don't forget to praise him."	216	_____
"Good boy, Zephyr," I said hastily.	222	_____

Needs Work 1 2 3 4 5 **Excellent**

Paid attention to punctuation

Needs Work 1 2 3 4 5 **Excellent**

Sounded good

Total Words Read _____

Total Errors – _____

Correct WPM _____

from *Adventure in Space:*

The Flight to Fix the Hubble

by Elaine Scott

First Reading

	Words Read	Miscues

If [the crew] didn't grab the Hubble on their first and only try,   13 _____

the mission would have failed before it began.   21 _____

    Claude was ready at the controls of the robot arm, waiting for   33 _____

the right moment. *Endeavor* glided into place below the telescope.   43 _____

Claude reached out with the mechanical arm and snared it! The   54 _____

telescope was safe, snugly tucked into the payload bay. With relief,   65 _____

Dick Covey radioed Mission Control. "Houston, *Endeavor* has a   74 _____

firm handshake with Mr. Hubble's telescope. It's quite a sight."   84 _____

The first crucial step of the repair mission was over. It was time   97 _____

for the space walks to begin.   103 _____

    Now the first surprise took its "bite." One of the solar arrays   115 _____

was badly twisted. Would it roll up as planned? Story and Jeff   127 _____

would look more closely the next day, when the "house calls" on   139 _____

Hubble would begin. Commander Dick Covey summed up the   148 _____

spirit of the crew when he said, "We are ready. We are inspired.   161 _____

Let's go fix this thing."   166 _____

    The next day, Kathy and Tom helped Story and Jeff put on   178 _____

their space suits. Their very lives would depend on them. Outer   189 _____

space is just that—space. It is a void. There is nothing in it.   203 _____

Needs Work   1   2   3   4   5   Excellent
     Paid attention to punctuation

Needs Work   1   2   3   4   5   Excellent
     Sounded good

Total Words Read   _____

Total Errors − _____

Correct WPM   _____

from *Adventure in Space:*
The Flight to Fix the Hubble
by Elaine Scott

Second Reading

	Words Read	Miscues

If [the crew] didn't grab the Hubble on their first and only try, — 13 _____

the mission would have failed before it began. — 21 _____

    Claude was ready at the controls of the robot arm, waiting for — 33 _____

the right moment. *Endeavor* glided into place below the telescope. — 43 _____

Claude reached out with the mechanical arm and snared it! The — 54 _____

telescope was safe, snugly tucked into the payload bay. With relief, — 65 _____

Dick Covey radioed Mission Control. "Houston, *Endeavor* has a — 74 _____

firm handshake with Mr. Hubble's telescope. It's quite a sight." — 84 _____

The first crucial step of the repair mission was over. It was time — 97 _____

for the space walks to begin. — 103 _____

    Now the first surprise took its "bite." One of the solar arrays — 115 _____

was badly twisted. Would it roll up as planned? Story and Jeff — 127 _____

would look more closely the next day, when the "house calls" on — 139 _____

Hubble would begin. Commander Dick Covey summed up the — 148 _____

spirit of the crew when he said, "We are ready. We are inspired. — 161 _____

Let's go fix this thing." — 166 _____

    The next day, Kathy and Tom helped Story and Jeff put on — 178 _____

their space suits. Their very lives would depend on them. Outer — 189 _____

space is just that—space. It is a void. There is nothing in it. — 203 _____

Needs Work   1   2   3   4   5   Excellent
     Paid attention to punctuation

Needs Work   1   2   3   4   5   Excellent
     Sounded good

Total Words Read _____

Total Errors − _____

Correct WPM _____

9 from "Your Mind Is a Mirror"
by Joan Aiken

Fiction

First Reading

	Words Read	Miscues

"Ah, I see." She reflected in silence for a moment. Then she | 12 | _____

told Sam, "Well, it is still possible for you to return it. That will | 26 | _____

mean going into the past." | 31 | _____

"Into the past? How in the world can I do that?" | 42 | _____

"You must go back precisely to the point at which you took the | 55 | _____

book. Not a moment sooner, not a moment later. Put the book | 67 | _____

down on the beach where you picked it up." | 76 | _____

"How can I get there?" | 81 | _____

"You go backwards," explained Madame Bonamy. "That is not | 90 | _____

difficult. Write with this diamond pencil on the looking-glass. | 99 | _____

Write very small. First, place the book under the glass—so." | 110 | _____

Sam, who had got out of bed, took the diamond pencil from | 122 | _____

her and stood before the mirror on the dressing-table. Simon the | 133 | _____

cat, uncurling himself, yawning, stretching, followed Sam. | 140 | _____

"What shall I write?" | 144 | _____

"You must write in backwards writing, beginning at the bottom | 154 | _____

right-hand corner. Each word back to front. Each sentence back to | 165 | _____

front. You must write everything that you did, every single thing | 176 | _____

that you have done today, backwards, beginning at the last minute | 187 | _____

before you got into bed." | 192 | _____

"I see." Sam thought for a minute, then lifted his hand towards | 204 | _____

the glass. | 206 | _____

Needs Work   1   2   3   4   5   Excellent
Paid attention to punctuation

Needs Work   1   2   3   4   5   Excellent
Sounded good

Total Words Read _____

Total Errors − _____

Correct WPM _____

from "Your Mind Is a Mirror"

by Joan Aiken

	Words Read	Miscues
"Ah, I see." She reflected in silence for a moment. Then she	12	_____
told Sam, "Well, it is still possible for you to return it. That will	26	_____
mean going into the past."	31	_____
"Into the past? How in the world can I do that?"	42	_____
"You must go back precisely to the point at which you took the	55	_____
book. Not a moment sooner, not a moment later. Put the book	67	_____
down on the beach where you picked it up."	76	_____
"How can I get there?"	81	_____
"You go backwards," explained Madame Bonamy. "That is not	90	_____
difficult. Write with this diamond pencil on the looking-glass.	99	_____
Write very small. First, place the book under the glass—so."	110	_____
Sam, who had got out of bed, took the diamond pencil from	122	_____
her and stood before the mirror on the dressing-table. Simon the	133	_____
cat, uncurling himself, yawning, stretching, followed Sam.	140	_____
"What shall I write?"	144	_____
"You must write in backwards writing, beginning at the bottom	154	_____
right-hand corner. Each word back to front. Each sentence back to	165	_____
front. You must write everything that you did, every single thing	176	_____
that you have done today, backwards, beginning at the last minute	187	_____
before you got into bed."	192	_____
"I see." Sam thought for a minute, then lifted his hand towards	204	_____
the glass.	206	_____

Needs Work   1 2 3 4 5   Excellent
Paid attention to punctuation

Needs Work   1 2 3 4 5   Excellent
Sounded good

Total Words Read   _____

Total Errors   − _____

Correct WPM   _____

10 from *To Kill a Mockingbird*
by Harper Lee

Fiction

First Reading

	Words Read	Miscues

Jem skipped two steps, put his foot on the porch, heaved himself | 12 | _____

to it, and teetered a long moment. He regained his balance and | 24 | _____

dropped to his knees. He crawled to the window, raised his head | 36 | _____

and looked in. | 39 | _____

Then I saw the shadow. It was the shadow of a man with a hat | 54 | _____

on. At first I thought it was a tree, but there was no wind blowing, | 69 | _____

and tree-trunks never walked. The back porch was bathed in | 79 | _____

moonlight, and the shadow, crisp as toast, moved across the porch | 90 | _____

toward Jem. | 92 | _____

Dill saw it next. He put his hands to his face. | 103 | _____

When it crossed Jem, Jem saw it. He put his arms over his | 116 | _____

head and went rigid. | 120 | _____

The shadow stopped about a foot beyond Jem. Its arm came | 131 | _____

out from its side, dropped, and was still. Then it turned and | 143 | _____

moved back across Jem, walked along the porch and off the side | 155 | _____

of the house, returning as it had come. | 163 | _____

Jem leaped off the porch and galloped toward us. He flung | 174 | _____

open the gate, danced Dill and me through, and shooed us | 185 | _____

between two rows of swishing collards. Halfway through the | 194 | _____

collards I tripped; as I tripped the roar of a shotgun shattered | 206 | _____

the neighborhood. | 208 | _____

Needs Work   1   2   3   4   5   Excellent
Paid attention to punctuation

Needs Work   1   2   3   4   5   Excellent
Sounded good

Total Words Read _____

Total Errors − _____

Correct WPM _____

from ***To Kill a Mockingbird***

by Harper Lee

	Words Read	Miscues

Jem skipped two steps, put his foot on the porch, heaved himself   12 _____

to it, and teetered a long moment. He regained his balance and   24 _____

dropped to his knees. He crawled to the window, raised his head   36 _____

and looked in.   39 _____

Then I saw the shadow. It was the shadow of a man with a hat   54 _____

on. At first I thought it was a tree, but there was no wind blowing,   69 _____

and tree-trunks never walked. The back porch was bathed in   79 _____

moonlight, and the shadow, crisp as toast, moved across the porch   90 _____

toward Jem.   92 _____

Dill saw it next. He put his hands to his face.   103 _____

When it crossed Jem, Jem saw it. He put his arms over his   116 _____

head and went rigid.   120 _____

The shadow stopped about a foot beyond Jem. Its arm came   131 _____

out from its side, dropped, and was still. Then it turned and   143 _____

moved back across Jem, walked along the porch and off the side   155 _____

of the house, returning as it had come.   163 _____

Jem leaped off the porch and galloped toward us. He flung   174 _____

open the gate, danced Dill and me through, and shooed us   185 _____

between two rows of swishing collards. Halfway through the   194 _____

collards I tripped; as I tripped the roar of a shotgun shattered   206 _____

the neighborhood.   208 _____

Needs Work   1   2   3   4   5   Excellent
Paid attention to punctuation

Needs Work   1   2   3   4   5   Excellent
Sounded good

Total Words Read _____

Total Errors – _____

Correct WPM _____

11 from **"The Circuit"**
by Francisco Jiménez

Fiction

First Reading

	Words Read	Miscues

‿‿‿

At sunset we drove into a labor camp near Fresno. Since Papá   12   _____

did not speak English, Mamá asked the camp foreman if he   23   _____

needed any more workers. "We don't need no more," said the   34   _____

foreman, scratching his head. "Check with Sullivan down the   43   _____

road. Can't miss him. He lives in a big white house with a fence   57   _____

around it."   59   _____

When we got there, Mamá walked up to the house. She went   71   _____

through a white gate, past a row of rose bushes, up the stairs to   85   _____

the front door. She rang the doorbell. The porch light went on   97   _____

and a tall husky man came out. They exchanged a few words.   109   _____

After the man went in, Mamá clasped her hands and hurried back   121   _____

to the car. "We have work! Mr. Sullivan said we can stay there the   135   _____

whole season," she said, gasping and pointing to an old garage   146   _____

near the stables.   149   _____

The garage was worn out by the years. It had no windows. The   162   _____

walls, eaten by termites, strained to support the roof full of holes.   174   _____

The dirt floor, populated by earth worms, looked like a gray road   186   _____

map. That night, by the light of a kerosene lamp, we unpacked   198   _____

and cleaned our new home.   203   _____

Needs Work   1 2 3 4 5   Excellent
Paid attention to punctuation

Needs Work   1 2 3 4 5   Excellent
Sounded good

Total Words Read   _____

Total Errors   − _____

Correct WPM   _____

from "The Circuit"
by Francisco Jiménez

	Words Read	Miscues
At sunset we drove into a labor camp near Fresno. Since Papá	12	_____
did not speak English, Mamá asked the camp foreman if he	23	_____
needed any more workers. "We don't need no more," said the	34	_____
foreman, scratching his head. "Check with Sullivan down the	43	_____
road. Can't miss him. He lives in a big white house with a fence	57	_____
around it."	59	_____
When we got there, Mamá walked up to the house. She went	71	_____
through a white gate, past a row of rose bushes, up the stairs to	85	_____
the front door. She rang the doorbell. The porch light went on	97	_____
and a tall husky man came out. They exchanged a few words.	109	_____
After the man went in, Mamá clasped her hands and hurried back	121	_____
to the car. "We have work! Mr. Sullivan said we can stay there the	135	_____
whole season," she said, gasping and pointing to an old garage	146	_____
near the stables.	149	_____
The garage was worn out by the years. It had no windows. The	162	_____
walls, eaten by termites, strained to support the roof full of holes.	174	_____
The dirt floor, populated by earth worms, looked like a gray road	186	_____
map. That night, by the light of a kerosene lamp, we unpacked	198	_____
and cleaned our new home.	203	_____

Needs Work   1   2   3   4   5   Excellent
Paid attention to punctuation

Needs Work   1   2   3   4   5   Excellent
Sounded good

Total Words Read _____

Total Errors − _____

Correct WPM _____

12 from *Number the Stars*
by Lois Lowry
Fiction

	Words Read	Miscues

Annemarie looked up, panting, just as she reached the corner. | 10 | _____

Her laughter stopped. Her heart seemed to skip a beat. | 20 | _____

"*Halte!*" the soldier ordered in a stern voice. | 28 | _____

The German word was as familiar as it was frightening. | 38 | _____

Annemarie had heard it often enough before, but it had never | 49 | _____

been directed at her until now. | 55 | _____

Behind her, Ellen also slowed and stopped. Far back, little | 65 | _____

Kirsti was plodding along, her face in a pout because the girls | 77 | _____

hadn't waited for her. | 81 | _____

Annemarie stared up. There were two of them. That meant | 91 | _____

two helmets, two sets of cold eyes glaring at her, and four tall | 104 | _____

shiny boots planted firmly on the sidewalk, blocking her path | 114 | _____

to home. | 116 | _____

And it meant two rifles, gripped in the hands of the soldiers. | 128 | _____

She stared at the rifles first. Then, finally, she looked into the face | 141 | _____

of the soldier who had ordered her to halt. | 150 | _____

"Why are you running?" the harsh voice asked. His Danish | 160 | _____

was very poor. Three years, Annemarie thought with contempt. | 169 | _____

Three years they've been in our country, and still they can't speak | 181 | _____

our language. | 183 | _____

"I was racing with my friend," she answered politely. "We have | 194 | _____

races at school every Friday, and I want to do well, so I—" Her | 208 | _____

voice trailed away, the sentence unfinished. | 214 | _____

Needs Work   1   2   3   4   5   Excellent
        Paid attention to punctuation

Needs Work   1   2   3   4   5   Excellent
        Sounded good

Total Words Read _____

Total Errors − _____

Correct WPM _____

23

from *Number the Stars*

by Lois Lowry

	Words Read	Miscues

Annemarie looked up, panting, just as she reached the corner. | 10 | _____ |

Her laughter stopped. Her heart seemed to skip a beat. | 20 | _____ |

"*Halte!*" the soldier ordered in a stern voice. | 28 | _____ |

The German word was as familiar as it was frightening. | 38 | _____ |

Annemarie had heard it often enough before, but it had never | 49 | _____ |

been directed at her until now. | 55 | _____ |

Behind her, Ellen also slowed and stopped. Far back, little | 65 | _____ |

Kirsti was plodding along, her face in a pout because the girls | 77 | _____ |

hadn't waited for her. | 81 | _____ |

Annemarie stared up. There were two of them. That meant | 91 | _____ |

two helmets, two sets of cold eyes glaring at her, and four tall | 104 | _____ |

shiny boots planted firmly on the sidewalk, blocking her path | 114 | _____ |

to home. | 116 | _____ |

And it meant two rifles, gripped in the hands of the soldiers. | 128 | _____ |

She stared at the rifles first. Then, finally, she looked into the face | 141 | _____ |

of the soldier who had ordered her to halt. | 150 | _____ |

"Why are you running?" the harsh voice asked. His Danish | 160 | _____ |

was very poor. Three years, Annemarie thought with contempt. | 169 | _____ |

Three years they've been in our country, and still they can't speak | 181 | _____ |

our language. | 183 | _____ |

"I was racing with my friend," she answered politely. "We have | 194 | _____ |

races at school every Friday, and I want to do well, so I—" Her | 208 | _____ |

voice trailed away, the sentence unfinished. | 214 | _____ |

Needs Work   1 2 3 4 5   Excellent
Paid attention to punctuation

Needs Work   1 2 3 4 5   Excellent
Sounded good

Total Words Read _____

Total Errors – _____

Correct WPM _____

24

13

Fiction

from *Addie Across the Prairie*
by Laurie Lawlor

First Reading

	Words Read	Miscues

Slowly, she lowered herself, balancing Burt [on her back] with   10 _____
great effort. Down into the well she went, step over step. Now   22 _____
they were below ground level. It was pitch black, and the water   34 _____
felt cold around Addie's knees as she reached the bottom rung.   45 _____
"Don't let go, Burt. Don't let go," she told her brother, who buried   58 _____
his face into the back of her neck so that her necklace dug deep   72 _____
into her skin.   75 _____

    The terrible roar of the fire grew louder. Addie wanted to   86 _____
cover both her ears, but she could not let go. She had to hold on   101 _____
tight to the ladder while standing as still as possible. Any minute   113 _____
the fire would be right over them. What would happen then?   124 _____
Would they melt? She remained motionless even as several stones   134 _____
and a handful of dirt came loose from the wall and tumbled into   147 _____
the water. Was the well going to cave in on them?   158 _____

    Now the noise was deafening. Pieces of burning grass hissed   168 _____
as they fell into the well water, just missing the children. Cinders   180 _____
smarted Addie's eyes. How long? How long until the fire came?   191 _____
Addie glanced up just as the flames roared over the mouth of   203 _____
the well.   205 _____

Needs Work   1   2   3   4   5   Excellent
     Paid attention to punctuation

Needs Work   1   2   3   4   5   Excellent
     Sounded good

Total Words Read   _____

Total Errors   − _____

Correct WPM   _____

13

Fiction

from *Addie Across the Prairie*
by Laurie Lawlor

	Words Read	Miscues

Slowly, she lowered herself, balancing Burt [on her back] with | 10 | _____
great effort. Down into the well she went, step over step. Now | 22 | _____
they were below ground level. It was pitch black, and the water | 34 | _____
felt cold around Addie's knees as she reached the bottom rung. | 45 | _____
"Don't let go, Burt. Don't let go," she told her brother, who buried | 58 | _____
his face into the back of her neck so that her necklace dug deep | 72 | _____
into her skin. | 75 | _____

    The terrible roar of the fire grew louder. Addie wanted to | 86 | _____
cover both her ears, but she could not let go. She had to hold on | 101 | _____
tight to the ladder while standing as still as possible. Any minute | 113 | _____
the fire would be right over them. What would happen then? | 124 | _____
Would they melt? She remained motionless even as several stones | 134 | _____
and a handful of dirt came loose from the wall and tumbled into | 147 | _____
the water. Was the well going to cave in on them? | 158 | _____

    Now the noise was deafening. Pieces of burning grass hissed | 168 | _____
as they fell into the well water, just missing the children. Cinders | 180 | _____
smarted Addie's eyes. How long? How long until the fire came? | 191 | _____
Addie glanced up just as the flames roared over the mouth of | 203 | _____
the well. | 205 | _____

Needs Work 1 2 3 4 5 Excellent
Paid attention to punctuation

Needs Work 1 2 3 4 5 Excellent
Sounded good

Total Words Read _____

Total Errors − _____

Correct WPM _____

from *Outlaw Red*

by Jim Kjelgaard

Fiction

First Reading

	Words Read	Miscues

The trap was stronger than [the dog, Sean].   8   _____

Wet fur plastered close against his body, his long hair dripping   19   _____
icy water, Sean bent his head to look again at the trap. It was a   34   _____
puzzle, a cold and unyielding thing with no life or being of its   47   _____
own. He had already discovered that he could not rend it with   59   _____
his jaws or pull himself out of it. Still, there must be a way.   73   _____

He laid his trapped paw on the boulder, beside the dead hare.   85   _____
Carefully he pulled the big snowshoe over the trap, so that it was   98   _____
completely hidden. He tried to walk away. When he did, the trap   110   _____
came with him. Apparently it could not be hidden. Sean nosed   121   _____
his swelling paw, and licked it gently with a warm tongue.   132   _____

Suddenly he tensed himself and bristled. The eddying winds   141   _____
had brought to him the faint scent of man.   150   _____

Sean sat down on the boulder and waited. Fear and uncertainty   161   _____
tore at him. He had a great desire to run, but he could not because   176   _____
the trap held him fast. Five minutes later he saw the man.   188   _____

Billy Dash stood framed in the hemlocks.   195   _____

Needs Work   1   2   3   4   5   Excellent
Paid attention to punctuation

Needs Work   1   2   3   4   5   Excellent
Sounded good

Total Words Read _____

Total Errors − _____

Correct WPM _____

from *Outlaw Red*
by Jim Kjelgaard

	Words Read	Miscues

The trap was stronger than [the dog, Sean]. — 8 _____

Wet fur plastered close against his body, his long hair dripping 19 _____
icy water, Sean bent his head to look again at the trap. It was a 34 _____
puzzle, a cold and unyielding thing with no life or being of its 47 _____
own. He had already discovered that he could not rend it with 59 _____
his jaws or pull himself out of it. Still, there must be a way. 73 _____

He laid his trapped paw on the boulder, beside the dead hare. 85 _____
Carefully he pulled the big snowshoe over the trap, so that it was 98 _____
completely hidden. He tried to walk away. When he did, the trap 110 _____
came with him. Apparently it could not be hidden. Sean nosed 121 _____
his swelling paw, and licked it gently with a warm tongue. 132 _____

Suddenly he tensed himself and bristled. The eddying winds 141 _____
had brought to him the faint scent of man. 150 _____

Sean sat down on the boulder and waited. Fear and uncertainty 161 _____
tore at him. He had a great desire to run, but he could not because 176 _____
the trap held him fast. Five minutes later he saw the man. 188 _____

Billy Dash stood framed in the hemlocks. 195 _____

Needs Work   1   2   3   4   5   Excellent
Paid attention to punctuation

Needs Work   1   2   3   4   5   Excellent
Sounded good

Total Words Read   _____

Total Errors   − _____

Correct WPM   _____

from *Across the Wild River*
by Bill Gutman

Fiction

First Reading

	Words Read	Miscues

The breakaway herd kept coming and was now less than a | 11 | _____

hundred yards from the [wagon] train. | 17 | _____

"*Form two lines!*" Colonel Stewart shouted, waving a saber in | 27 | _____

the air. "*Load your weapons and aim for the leaders!*" | 37 | _____

The men in front dropped to one knee. James saw that [his | 49 | _____

friend] Will was among them. The men in the second line stood. | 61 | _____

Pa was standing, the last man on the left side. | 71 | _____

"*Fire!*" the colonel screamed. | 75 | _____

The guns sounded at once. A line of smoke rose, was caught | 87 | _____

by the breeze, and scattered. Several of the lead buffalo stumbled | 98 | _____

for a stride or two, but only one of them fell. James could see | 112 | _____

spots of red on the ones that had stumbled. | 121 | _____

Some of the men had brought more than one rifle. They quickly | 133 | _____

fired them. Again only one buffalo fell. | 140 | _____

"*Reload!*" | 141 | _____

The buffalo kept coming. James stood behind the wagons and | 151 | _____

prayed, his heart in his throat. | 157 | _____

"*Fire!*" | 158 | _____

This time the two lead buffalo, which had already been | 168 | _____

wounded, dropped and rolled. The ones behind them dodged the | 178 | _____

fallen bodies and kept coming. The buffalo would be on top of | 190 | _____

the men before they could reload and get off another volley. | 201 | _____

Needs Work   1   2   3   4   5   Excellent
Paid attention to punctuation

Needs Work   1   2   3   4   5   Excellent
Sounded good

Total Words Read _____

Total Errors − _____

Correct WPM _____

15

Fiction

from *Across the Wild River*

by Bill Gutman

	Words Read	Miscues
The breakaway herd kept coming and was now less than a	11	_____
hundred yards from the [wagon] train.	17	_____
"*Form two lines!*" Colonel Stewart shouted, waving a saber in	27	_____
the air. "*Load your weapons and aim for the leaders!*"	37	_____
The men in front dropped to one knee. James saw that [his	49	_____
friend] Will was among them. The men in the second line stood.	61	_____
Pa was standing, the last man on the left side.	71	_____
"*Fire!*" the colonel screamed.	75	_____
The guns sounded at once. A line of smoke rose, was caught	87	_____
by the breeze, and scattered. Several of the lead buffalo stumbled	98	_____
for a stride or two, but only one of them fell. James could see	112	_____
spots of red on the ones that had stumbled.	121	_____
Some of the men had brought more than one rifle. They quickly	133	_____
fired them. Again only one buffalo fell.	140	_____
"*Reload!*"	141	_____
The buffalo kept coming. James stood behind the wagons and	151	_____
prayed, his heart in his throat.	157	_____
"*Fire!*"	158	_____
This time the two lead buffalo, which had already been	168	_____
wounded, dropped and rolled. The ones behind them dodged the	178	_____
fallen bodies and kept coming. The buffalo would be on top of	190	_____
the men before they could reload and get off another volley.	201	_____

Needs Work   1   2   3   4   5   Excellent
Paid attention to punctuation

Needs Work   1   2   3   4   5   Excellent
Sounded good

Total Words Read   _____

Total Errors   −_____

Correct WPM   _____

16

Fiction

from *The Wind in the Willows*

by Kenneth Grahame

	Words Read	Miscues

"The Badger and I have been round and round the place, by night | 13 | _____ |

and by day; always the same thing. Sentries posted everywhere, | 23 | _____ |

guns poked out at us, stones thrown at us; always an animal on | 36 | _____ |

the look-out, and when they see us, my! how they do laugh! That's | 49 | _____ |

what annoys me most!" [said the Mole.] | 56 | _____ |

"It's a very difficult situation," said the Rat, reflecting deeply. | 66 | _____ |

"But I think I see now, in the depths of my mind, what Toad really | 81 | _____ |

ought to do. I will tell you. He ought to—" | 91 | _____ |

"No, he oughtn't!" shouted the Mole, with his mouth full. | 101 | _____ |

"Nothing of the sort! You don't understand. What he ought to do | 113 | _____ |

is, he ought to—" | 117 | _____ |

"Well, I shan't do it, anyway!" cried Toad, getting excited. "I'm | 128 | _____ |

not going to be ordered about by you fellows! It's my house we're | 141 | _____ |

talking about, and I know exactly what to do, and I'll tell you. I'm | 155 | _____ |

going to—" | 157 | _____ |

By this time they were all three talking at once, at the top of | 171 | _____ |

their voices, and the noise was simply deafening, when a thin, dry | 183 | _____ |

voice made itself heard, saying, "Be quiet at once, all of you!" and | 196 | _____ |

instantly every one was silent. | 201 | _____ |

Needs Work   1   2   3   4   5   Excellent
        Paid attention to punctuation

Needs Work   1   2   3   4   5   Excellent
        Sounded good

Total Words Read _____

Total Errors − _____

Correct WPM _____

16

from *The Wind in the Willows*
by Kenneth Grahame

Second Reading

	Words Read	Miscues

"The Badger and I have been round and round the place, by night **13** _____

and by day; always the same thing. Sentries posted everywhere, **23** _____

guns poked out at us, stones thrown at us; always an animal on **36** _____

the look-out, and when they see us, my! how they do laugh! That's **49** _____

what annoys me most!" [said the Mole.] **56** _____

"It's a very difficult situation," said the Rat, reflecting deeply. **66** _____

"But I think I see now, in the depths of my mind, what Toad really **81** _____

ought to do. I will tell you. He ought to—" **91** _____

"No, he oughtn't!" shouted the Mole, with his mouth full. **101** _____

"Nothing of the sort! You don't understand. What he ought to do **113** _____

is, he ought to—" **117** _____

"Well, I shan't do it, anyway!" cried Toad, getting excited. "I'm **128** _____

not going to be ordered about by you fellows! It's my house we're **141** _____

talking about, and I know exactly what to do, and I'll tell you. I'm **155** _____

going to—" **157** _____

By this time they were all three talking at once, at the top of **171** _____

their voices, and the noise was simply deafening, when a thin, dry **183** _____

voice made itself heard, saying, "Be quiet at once, all of you!" and **196** _____

instantly every one was silent. **201** _____

Needs Work   1   2   3   4   5   Excellent
Paid attention to punctuation

Needs Work   1   2   3   4   5   Excellent
Sounded good

Total Words Read _____

Total Errors − _____

Correct WPM _____

17

Nonfiction

from *Biography of a Killer Whale*
by Barbara Steiner

	Words Read	Miscues
The whale pod swam close to an island. The bull male led the	13	_____
way. The females surrounded the two calves and followed slowly.	23	_____
The adult whales were always hungry. Sometimes they ate	32	_____
large fish or squid that happened to swim close. But they preferred	44	_____
warm-blooded animals such as seals, dolphins, and other whales.	53	_____
Karok still had no teeth, but the mature whales' jaws were designed	65	_____
for hunting. Karok's mother had twenty-four sharp teeth in each	75	_____
jaw. When she closed her mouth the teeth interlocked. His father	86	_____
was older. Some of his teeth were worn down, but they were still	99	_____
strong and useful.	102	_____
Karok's father clicked rapidly. He darted toward the rocky	111	_____
shore. An old elephant seal had dragged himself into the water to	123	_____
cool off. He was slow and careless. He was also wounded from	135	_____
fighting off younger seals. . . .	139	_____
The elephant seal never saw the black shadow zooming toward	149	_____
him. The huge killer whale surfaced. He tossed the two-ton seal	160	_____
into the air. Then he dived, carrying the seal into deeper water.	172	_____
His teeth closed down. The other whales swam closer to eat what	184	_____
was left.	186	_____
The whale pod swam near the rocky coast all day. But the	198	_____
other elephant seals knew the whales were hunting.	206	_____
At dusk the killer whales started toward deeper water.	215	_____

Needs Work   1   2   3   4   5   Excellent
_____
Paid attention to punctuation

Needs Work   1   2   3   4   5   Excellent
_____
Sounded good

Total Words Read   _____

Total Errors − _____

Correct WPM   _____

from *Biography of a Killer Whale*
by Barbara Steiner

	Words Read	Miscues
The whale pod swam close to an island. The bull male led the	13	_____
way. The females surrounded the two calves and followed slowly.	23	_____
The adult whales were always hungry. Sometimes they ate	32	_____
large fish or squid that happened to swim close. But they preferred	44	_____
warm-blooded animals such as seals, dolphins, and other whales.	53	_____
Karok still had no teeth, but the mature whales' jaws were designed	65	_____
for hunting. Karok's mother had twenty-four sharp teeth in each	75	_____
jaw. When she closed her mouth the teeth interlocked. His father	86	_____
was older. Some of his teeth were worn down, but they were still	99	_____
strong and useful.	102	_____
Karok's father clicked rapidly. He darted toward the rocky	111	_____
shore. An old elephant seal had dragged himself into the water to	123	_____
cool off. He was slow and careless. He was also wounded from	135	_____
fighting off younger seals. . . .	139	_____
The elephant seal never saw the black shadow zooming toward	149	_____
him. The huge killer whale surfaced. He tossed the two-ton seal	160	_____
into the air. Then he dived, carrying the seal into deeper water.	172	_____
His teeth closed down. The other whales swam closer to eat what	184	_____
was left.	186	_____
The whale pod swam near the rocky coast all day. But the	198	_____
other elephant seals knew the whales were hunting.	206	_____
At dusk the killer whales started toward deeper water.	215	_____

Needs Work   1 2 3 4 5   Excellent
Paid attention to punctuation

Needs Work   1 2 3 4 5   Excellent
Sounded good

Total Words Read _____

Total Errors – _____

Correct WPM _____

18 Freeing Keiko

Nonfiction

	Words Read	Miscues

The whale leaps into the air. Water streams down its back   11   _____

and splashes in thunderous spray. The whale is airborne. Will it   22   _____

escape? Can the boy "free Willy"?   28   _____

    The exciting movie *Free Willy* came out in 1993. Viewers were   39   _____

moved as they watched the story unfold on the screen. Fans   50   _____

wanted to learn more about the real whale who "played" the role   62   _____

of Willy. Just who was this movie's star?   70   _____

    It was a whale named Keiko. And fans soon learned that Keiko   82   _____

had a life story all his own.   89   _____

    In 1979 Keiko was a young whale. He traveled with his pod   101   _____

through the waters of the Atlantic. Then one day he swam into a   114   _____

fishing net. He was captured.   119   _____

    At first he lived in an aquarium in Iceland. After three years,   131   _____

he was moved to Marineland in Canada. When he did not seem   143   _____

to be doing well there, he was sold again. Now he lived in a small   158   _____

tank in an amusement park in Mexico City.   166   _____

    There, he was "discovered" by movie talent scouts. They chose   176   _____

him to star in *Free Willy*. After the movie's release, people's   187   _____

interest in Keiko would cause his life to change yet again. He   199   _____

would be freed, and he would return to live in the ocean again.   212   _____

Needs Work   1   2   3   4   5   Excellent
     Paid attention to punctuation

Needs Work   1   2   3   4   5   Excellent
     Sounded good

Total Words Read   _____

Total Errors   – _____

Correct WPM   _____

Freeing Keiko

	Words Read	Miscues
The whale leaps into the air. Water streams down its back	11	_____
and splashes in thunderous spray. The whale is airborne. Will it	22	_____
escape? Can the boy "free Willy"?	28	_____
The exciting movie *Free Willy* came out in 1993. Viewers were	39	_____
moved as they watched the story unfold on the screen. Fans	50	_____
wanted to learn more about the real whale who "played" the role	62	_____
of Willy. Just who was this movie's star?	70	_____
It was a whale named Keiko. And fans soon learned that Keiko	82	_____
had a life story all his own.	89	_____
In 1979 Keiko was a young whale. He traveled with his pod	101	_____
through the waters of the Atlantic. Then one day he swam into a	114	_____
fishing net. He was captured.	119	_____
At first he lived in an aquarium in Iceland. After three years,	131	_____
he was moved to Marineland in Canada. When he did not seem	143	_____
to be doing well there, he was sold again. Now he lived in a small	158	_____
tank in an amusement park in Mexico City.	166	_____
There, he was "discovered" by movie talent scouts. They chose	176	_____
him to star in *Free Willy*. After the movie's release, people's	187	_____
interest in Keiko would cause his life to change yet again. He	199	_____
would be freed, and he would return to live in the ocean again.	212	_____

Needs Work 1 2 3 4 5 Excellent
  Paid attention to punctuation

Needs Work 1 2 3 4 5 Excellent
  Sounded good

Total Words Read _____

Total Errors − _____

Correct WPM _____

19

Nonfiction

from *Biography of a Giraffe*
by Alice L. Hopf

One night something alerted the herd. A menacing sound   9   _____
came to them. From quite near at hand they heard a low gurgle   22   _____
that rose into the shrill laugh of the hyena. It was answered from   35   _____
another direction. A pack of hyenas was out hunting! The giraffes   46   _____
began to move away. The leaf-spotted calf jumped up quickly.   56   _____
Only the mother giraffe was lying down. She began to get to her   69   _____
feet, but it was difficult. First she pulled her long neck back as far   83   _____
as she could. Then she thrust it forward. This motion got her to   96   _____
her front knees. Again her neck jerked back and forth as she got   109   _____
her hind legs up. A final jerk got her onto her front feet.   122   _____

But now the hyenas were closer. The young giraffe did not   133   _____
know what to do. He wanted to stay close to his mother, but he   147   _____
also wanted to run from the attacking beasts. Suddenly the big   158   _____
bull giraffe was with them. His huge body seemed to blot out the   171   _____
stars. He stood between the mother giraffe and the hyenas. He   182   _____
swung his long neck at them. He hit one attacker and sent it   195   _____
flying a dozen yards away.   200   _____

Needs Work   1   2   3   4   5   Excellent
Paid attention to punctuation

Needs Work   1   2   3   4   5   Excellent
Sounded good

Total Words Read   _____

Total Errors   −   _____

Correct WPM   _____

from *Biography of a Giraffe*
by Alice L. Hopf

	Words Read	Miscues

One night something alerted the herd. A menacing sound   9   _____

came to them. From quite near at hand they heard a low gurgle   22   _____

that rose into the shrill laugh of the hyena. It was answered from   35   _____

another direction. A pack of hyenas was out hunting! The giraffes   46   _____

began to move away. The leaf-spotted calf jumped up quickly.   56   _____

Only the mother giraffe was lying down. She began to get to her   69   _____

feet, but it was difficult. First she pulled her long neck back as far   83   _____

as she could. Then she thrust it forward. This motion got her to   96   _____

her front knees. Again her neck jerked back and forth as she got   109   _____

her hind legs up. A final jerk got her onto her front feet.   122   _____

But now the hyenas were closer. The young giraffe did not   133   _____

know what to do. He wanted to stay close to his mother, but he   147   _____

also wanted to run from the attacking beasts. Suddenly the big   158   _____

bull giraffe was with them. His huge body seemed to blot out the   171   _____

stars. He stood between the mother giraffe and the hyenas. He   182   _____

swung his long neck at them. He hit one attacker and sent it   195   _____

flying a dozen yards away.   200   _____

Needs Work   1   2   3   4   5   Excellent

Paid attention to punctuation

Needs Work   1   2   3   4   5   Excellent

Sounded good

Total Words Read   _____

Total Errors − _____

Correct WPM   _____

20

Nonfiction

from *Margaret Bourke-White*

by Catherine A. Welch

	Words Read	Miscues

Margaret [Bourke-White] was sent to England as the first | 9 | _____

American woman war reporter. This time, her pictures would | 18 | _____

be used by the United States Air Force and *Life* magazine. | 29 | _____

Margaret would now have the exciting job of taking pictures | 39 | _____

of men in battle. Margaret was thrilled to be working for the Air | 52 | _____

Force. She loved taking pictures from airplanes. She begged to fly | 63 | _____

with the bombers. But combat missions were dangerous—too | 72 | _____

dangerous for a woman, many people thought. The Air Force sent | 83 | _____

men reporters instead. | 86 | _____

But soon Margaret heard about secret plans for the next big | 97 | _____

battle. England and America were going to invade the coast of | 108 | _____

North Africa and attack German forces there. Margaret wanted | 117 | _____

to go along, and the Air Force let her. They sent her by sea. The | 132 | _____

night before they reached Africa, a torpedo struck Margaret's ship. | 142 | _____

While the troops and nurses marched to the lifeboats, | 151 | _____

Margaret scrambled to the top deck with one camera. The ship | 162 | _____

might sink. Margaret might die. But fear did not stop Margaret. | 173 | _____

She was busy trying to work. | 179 | _____

She glanced at the sky. It was dark, but the moon was bright. | 192 | _____

Was there enough light to take pictures? Suddenly a voice called | 203 | _____

out from the loudspeaker. "Abandon ship!" | 209 | _____

Needs Work   1 2 3 4 5   Excellent
Paid attention to punctuation

Needs Work   1 2 3 4 5   Excellent
Sounded good

Total Words Read _____

Total Errors − _____

Correct WPM _____

from *Margaret Bourke-White*
by Catherine A. Welch

	Words Read	Miscues
Margaret [Bourke-White] was sent to England as the first	9	_____
American woman war reporter. This time, her pictures would	18	_____
be used by the United States Air Force and *Life* magazine.	29	_____
Margaret would now have the exciting job of taking pictures	39	_____
of men in battle. Margaret was thrilled to be working for the Air	52	_____
Force. She loved taking pictures from airplanes. She begged to fly	63	_____
with the bombers. But combat missions were dangerous—too	72	_____
dangerous for a woman, many people thought. The Air Force sent	83	_____
men reporters instead.	86	_____
But soon Margaret heard about secret plans for the next big	97	_____
battle. England and America were going to invade the coast of	108	_____
North Africa and attack German forces there. Margaret wanted	117	_____
to go along, and the Air Force let her. They sent her by sea. The	132	_____
night before they reached Africa, a torpedo struck Margaret's ship.	142	_____
While the troops and nurses marched to the lifeboats,	151	_____
Margaret scrambled to the top deck with one camera. The ship	162	_____
might sink. Margaret might die. But fear did not stop Margaret.	173	_____
She was busy trying to work.	179	_____
She glanced at the sky. It was dark, but the moon was bright.	192	_____
Was there enough light to take pictures? Suddenly a voice called	203	_____
out from the loudspeaker. "Abandon ship!"	209	_____

Needs Work   1 2 3 4 5   Excellent
Paid attention to punctuation

Needs Work   1 2 3 4 5   Excellent
Sounded good

Total Words Read _____

Total Errors − _____

Correct WPM _____

21 The Last Great Race on Earth

Nonfiction

	Words Read	Miscues

Iditarod racers can be tall or short, young or old, men or women. — 13 ——

There's only one thing that they cannot be: cowards. If they are, — 25 ——

they will never survive this grueling 1,160-mile race. — 33 ——

    In this race, each racer travels alone on a sled pulled by dogs. — 46 ——

The goal is to get from one end of Alaska to the other as fast as — 62 ——

possible. That means all the racers—or *mushers,* as they are — 73 ——

called—push themselves and their dogs to the limit. Sometimes — 83 ——

dogs die along the way. Mushers know that they, too, might die. — 95 ——

Still, every year people return to run this "Last Great Race — 106 ——

on Earth." — 108 ——

    The race begins in the city of Anchorage. Mushers harness — 118 ——

their best sled dogs. They jump onto sleds packed with food and — 130 ——

other supplies. Then they head out. With luck, the first hours go — 142 ——

smoothly. The dogs find their pace. — 148 ——

    The race course follows an old mail route that used to pass — 160 ——

through Alaska's mining towns. But since the towns are mostly — 170 ——

deserted now, the race is one long trek through the wilderness. — 181 ——

Mushers stop at 18 checkpoints along the way. Otherwise, they — 191 ——

have no contact with the outside world until they reach the finish — 203 ——

line in Nome. — 206 ——

Needs Work   1   2   3   4   5   Excellent
Paid attention to punctuation

Needs Work   1   2   3   4   5   Excellent
Sounded good

Total Words Read   _____

Total Errors   – _____

Correct WPM   _____

The Last Great Race on Earth

	Words Read	Miscues

Iditarod racers can be tall or short, young or old, men or women. · 13 · _____

There's only one thing that they cannot be: cowards. If they are, · 25 · _____

they will never survive this grueling 1,160-mile race. · 33 · _____

In this race, each racer travels alone on a sled pulled by dogs. · 46 · _____

The goal is to get from one end of Alaska to the other as fast as · 62 · _____

possible. That means all the racers—or *mushers,* as they are · 73 · _____

called—push themselves and their dogs to the limit. Sometimes · 83 · _____

dogs die along the way. Mushers know that they, too, might die. · 95 · _____

Still, every year people return to run this "Last Great Race · 106 · _____

on Earth." · 108 · _____

The race begins in the city of Anchorage. Mushers harness · 118 · _____

their best sled dogs. They jump onto sleds packed with food and · 130 · _____

other supplies. Then they head out. With luck, the first hours go · 142 · _____

smoothly. The dogs find their pace. · 148 · _____

The race course follows an old mail route that used to pass · 160 · _____

through Alaska's mining towns. But since the towns are mostly · 170 · _____

deserted now, the race is one long trek through the wilderness. · 181 · _____

Mushers stop at 18 checkpoints along the way. Otherwise, they · 191 · _____

have no contact with the outside world until they reach the finish · 203 · _____

line in Nome. · 206 · _____

Needs Work 1 2 3 4 5 Excellent
_____
Paid attention to punctuation

Needs Work 1 2 3 4 5 Excellent
_____
Sounded good

Total Words Read _____

Total Errors − _____

Correct WPM _____

22 Secrets from the Desert

Nonfiction

It all started with a lively goat. At least, that's the way the	13	_____
story goes.	15	_____
The story comes from a shepherd boy in the Middle East. This	27	_____
boy lived in Jordan. One day, in 1947, he and his goats were out	41	_____
in the desert, near the Dead Sea. One of the goats scampered off.	54	_____
The boy saw it go into a cave. He threw a stone into the cave to	70	_____
scare the goat out. When the stone landed, the boy heard	81	_____
something break.	83	_____
The boy ran off and brought a friend back to the cave.	95	_____
Together they climbed into the dark, dry cave. There they saw	106	_____
what the stone had hit. Lying on the floor were some old	118	_____
pottery jars.	120	_____
These jars weren't just old—they were ancient. They were	130	_____
2,000 years old. Rolled up in the jars were some ragged documents	142	_____
as old as the jars.	147	_____
The boys did not know it then, but the documents were of	159	_____
great importance. They were the first part of the Dead Sea Scrolls.	171	_____
Later more scrolls and scroll scraps were found in other caves.	182	_____
Researchers and scientists call the Dead Sea Scrolls one of the	193	_____
greatest finds ever.	196	_____

Needs Work   1   2   3   4   5   Excellent
Paid attention to punctuation

Needs Work   1   2   3   4   5   Excellent
Sounded good

Total Words Read _____

Total Errors – _____

Correct WPM _____

Secrets from the Desert

	Words Read	Miscues
It all started with a lively goat. At least, that's the way the	13	_____
story goes.	15	_____
The story comes from a shepherd boy in the Middle East. This	27	_____
boy lived in Jordan. One day, in 1947, he and his goats were out	41	_____
in the desert, near the Dead Sea. One of the goats scampered off.	54	_____
The boy saw it go into a cave. He threw a stone into the cave to	70	_____
scare the goat out. When the stone landed, the boy heard	81	_____
something break.	83	_____
The boy ran off and brought a friend back to the cave.	95	_____
Together they climbed into the dark, dry cave. There they saw	106	_____
what the stone had hit. Lying on the floor were some old	118	_____
pottery jars.	120	_____
These jars weren't just old—they were ancient. They were	130	_____
2,000 years old. Rolled up in the jars were some ragged documents	142	_____
as old as the jars.	147	_____
The boys did not know it then, but the documents were of	159	_____
great importance. They were the first part of the Dead Sea Scrolls.	171	_____
Later more scrolls and scroll scraps were found in other caves.	182	_____
Researchers and scientists call the Dead Sea Scrolls one of the	193	_____
greatest finds ever.	196	_____

Needs Work   1   2   3   4   5   Excellent

Paid attention to punctuation

Needs Work   1   2   3   4   5   Excellent

Sounded good

Total Words Read _____

Total Errors – _____

Correct WPM _____

23

Nonfiction

Race Through the Sand

First Reading

	Words Read	Miscues

So you like to run? Then maybe the Marathon of the Sands is   13   _____
the race for you. Of course, you'll have to fly to Morocco. Once   26   _____
there, you'll have to run 140 miles in seven days. And you'll have   39   _____
to do it in 120°F heat.   45   _____

Organizers boast that the Marathon of the Sands is "the world's   56   _____
toughest footrace." It has six stages, each taking place in the hot   68   _____
Sahara Desert. Runners don't just run. They run in the sand. They   80   _____
don't just carry a water bottle. They carry on their backs all the   93   _____
goods that they will need over the course of the seven-day race.   105   _____
This means food, clothes, sleeping bags, compasses, and flares are   115   _____
packed in their backpacks. And, oh yes, each runner also carries a   127   _____
snakebite kit.   129   _____

The first Marathon of the Sands race was held in 1986. Each   141   _____
year, about 500 people sign up to run this race. Because of the   154   _____
harsh conditions, it would seem that many runners would perish.   164   _____
But since its start, only one runner has died.   173   _____

While most people don't die, they do pay a price. Many drop   185   _____
out of the race. Some are dehydrated. Some have heat exhaustion.   196   _____
Some collapse with sunstroke. And even those who finish wind   206   _____
up in pain.   209   _____

Needs Work   1   2   3   4   5   Excellent
Paid attention to punctuation

Needs Work   1   2   3   4   5   Excellent
Sounded good

Total Words Read   _____

Total Errors   – _____

Correct WPM   _____

Race Through the Sand

	Words Read	Miscues

So you like to run? Then maybe the Marathon of the Sands is **13** _____

the race for you. Of course, you'll have to fly to Morocco. Once **26** _____

there, you'll have to run 140 miles in seven days. And you'll have **39** _____

to do it in 120°F heat. **45** _____

Organizers boast that the Marathon of the Sands is "the world's **56** _____

toughest footrace." It has six stages, each taking place in the hot **68** _____

Sahara Desert. Runners don't just run. They run in the sand. They **80** _____

don't just carry a water bottle. They carry on their backs all the **93** _____

goods that they will need over the course of the seven-day race. **105** _____

This means food, clothes, sleeping bags, compasses, and flares are **115** _____

packed in their backpacks. And, oh yes, each runner also carries a **127** _____

snakebite kit. **129** _____

The first Marathon of the Sands race was held in 1986. Each **141** _____

year, about 500 people sign up to run this race. Because of the **154** _____

harsh conditions, it would seem that many runners would perish. **164** _____

But since its start, only one runner has died. **173** _____

While most people don't die, they do pay a price. Many drop **185** _____

out of the race. Some are dehydrated. Some have heat exhaustion. **196** _____

Some collapse with sunstroke. And even those who finish wind **206** _____

up in pain. **209** _____

Needs Work   1   2   3   4   5   Excellent
Paid attention to punctuation

Needs Work   1   2   3   4   5   Excellent
Sounded good

Total Words Read _____

Total Errors − _____

Correct WPM _____

24 from *Summer of the Monkeys*
by Wilson Rawls

Fiction

Rowdy had something treed in a huge bur oak that was a solid	13	_____
mass of green. As I walked around the big tree, I peered into the	27	_____
dark foliage.	29	_____
I said, "What is it, boy? A squirrel?"	37	_____
Not being able to see anything, I backed off to one side, picked	50	_____
up a stick, and threw it up into the branches. From a shadow	63	_____
close to the trunk of the big tree, something moved out on a limb.	77	_____
I couldn't see what it was until it walked into an opening.	89	_____
At first, I thought my eyes were playing tricks on me. I just	102	_____
couldn't believe what I was seeing. It was a monkey—an honest-	114	_____
to-goodness live monkey. I was so surprised I couldn't move or	124	_____
say a word. All I could do was stand there with my eyes bugged	138	_____
out, and stare at it.	143	_____
The monkey was staring at me, too. He just sat there on a	156	_____
limb, boring holes through me with his bright little eyes. Then he	168	_____
opened his mouth like he was going to scream his head off, but	181	_____
he didn't make a sound. All he did was show me a mouthful of	195	_____
needle-sharp teeth. He looked so cute and funny, I couldn't help	206	_____
laughing out loud.	209	_____
Rowdy had seen the monkey, too; and was having a hound	220	_____
dog fit.	222	_____

Needs Work   1   2   3   4   5   Excellent
Paid attention to punctuation

Needs Work   1   2   3   4   5   Excellent
Sounded good

Total Words Read _____

Total Errors − _____

Correct WPM _____

24

Fiction

from *Summer of the Monkeys*
by Wilson Rawls

Rowdy had something treed in a huge bur oak that was a solid	13 _____
mass of green. As I walked around the big tree, I peered into the	27 _____
dark foliage.	29 _____

Rowdy had something treed in a huge bur oak that was a solid mass of green. As I walked around the big tree, I peered into the dark foliage.

I said, "What is it, boy? A squirrel?"

Not being able to see anything, I backed off to one side, picked up a stick, and threw it up into the branches. From a shadow close to the trunk of the big tree, something moved out on a limb. I couldn't see what it was until it walked into an opening.

At first, I thought my eyes were playing tricks on me. I just couldn't believe what I was seeing. It was a monkey—an honest-to-goodness live monkey. I was so surprised I couldn't move or say a word. All I could do was stand there with my eyes bugged out, and stare at it.

The monkey was staring at me, too. He just sat there on a limb, boring holes through me with his bright little eyes. Then he opened his mouth like he was going to scream his head off, but he didn't make a sound. All he did was show me a mouthful of needle-sharp teeth. He looked so cute and funny, I couldn't help laughing out loud.

Rowdy had seen the monkey, too; and was having a hound dog fit.

37	
50	
63	
77	
89	
102	
114	
124	
138	
143	
156	
168	
181	
195	
206	
209	
220	
222	

Needs Work   1 2 3 4 5   Excellent
Paid attention to punctuation

Needs Work   1 2 3 4 5   Excellent
Sounded good

Total Words Read   _____

Total Errors − _____

Correct WPM   _____

25 Year of the Plague

Fiction

	Words Read	Miscues

————— ❊❊❊ —————

"Bring out your dead! Bring out your dead!" The wheels of the dead-cart rattled over the cobblestones outside the house. Molly trembled as she lay in bed next to her sister Meg. That summer of 1666, the plague held London in its iron grip. Each night the dead-cart rolled through the city, picking up the bodies of people who had died of the dreaded disease.

Molly heard her father stumble out of bed. Then she heard him groan and the creak of the bed as he lay back down. "William?" Molly heard her mother whisper. "Are you well, William?" Then came her father's reply. "No, Sarah. I am not well."

"Molly!" her mother called. Molly got out of bed and hurried to her mother. "You and your sister must run to your Aunt Emily's house. It will be safer there for both of you."

"Is it the plague, Mother?" Molly asked.

"Let us pray it is not," her mother said. "I will send for the doctor. But you must go now, before the doctor comes. If it is the plague, the watchmen will seal up the house with us inside. I must stay with your father."

Holding her little sister's hand, Molly hurried through the darkened streets. She tried to believe that it was not the plague, that her father would get well. Only time would tell.

Words Read
12
21
34
47
58
65
77
90
100
110
121
134
144
151
165
179
192
196
205
217
227

Needs Work   1   2   3   4   5   Excellent
Paid attention to punctuation

Needs Work   1   2   3   4   5   Excellent
Sounded good

Total Words Read _____

Total Errors − _____

Correct WPM _____

Year of the Plague

	Words Read	Miscues

"Bring out your dead! Bring out your dead!" The wheels of the   12   _____

dead-cart rattled over the cobblestones outside the house. Molly   21   _____

trembled as she lay in bed next to her sister Meg. That summer   34   _____

of 1666, the plague held London in its iron grip. Each night the   47   _____

dead-cart rolled through the city, picking up the bodies of people   58   _____

who had died of the dreaded disease.   65   _____

Molly heard her father stumble out of bed. Then she heard him   77   _____

groan and the creak of the bed as he lay back down. "William?"   90   _____

Molly heard her mother whisper. "Are you well, William?" Then   100   _____

came her father's reply. "No, Sarah. I am not well."   110   _____

"Molly!" her mother called. Molly got out of bed and hurried   121   _____

to her mother. "You and your sister must run to your Aunt Emily's   134   _____

house. It will be safer there for both of you."   144   _____

"Is it the plague, Mother?" Molly asked.   151   _____

"Let us pray it is not," her mother said. "I will send for the   165   _____

doctor. But you must go now, before the doctor comes. If it is the   179   _____

plague, the watchmen will seal up the house with us inside. I must   192   _____

stay with your father."   196   _____

Holding her little sister's hand, Molly hurried through the   205   _____

darkened streets. She tried to believe that it was not the plague,   217   _____

that her father would get well. Only time would tell.   227   _____

Needs Work   1   2   3   4   5   Excellent
Paid attention to punctuation

Needs Work   1   2   3   4   5   Excellent
Sounded good

Total Words Read   _____

Total Errors   − _____

Correct WPM   _____

26 from *Heidi*
Fiction
by Johanna Spyri

	Words Read	Miscues

Dete stood still. A stout, kind-looking woman came out of the   11   _____

house and joined them. "Where are you taking the child, Dete?"   22   _____

she asked. "I suppose it is your sister's child—the orphan?"   33   _____

"Yes," answered Dete. "I am taking her to stay with Alm-Uncle."   44   _____

"Surely you aren't going to leave the child with *him*. You must   56   _____

be out of your mind, Dete! But the old man is sure to turn you   71   _____

away, in any case!"   75   _____

"He can't do that! After all, he is her grandfather. I have looked   88   _____

after the child up till now, and I can tell you, Barbel, I am not   103   _____

going to turn down the offer of a good job on her account. From   117   _____

now on the grandfather will have to do his bit as well."   129   _____

"Oh, well, if he were like other people—" replied Barbel, "but   140   _____

you know him as well as I do. How can he look after a child, and   156   _____

especially such a little one? Oh, she will never stay with him! But   169   _____

where are *you* going, Dete?"   174   _____

"To a very good job in Frankfurt," explained Dete.   183   _____

"Well, I certainly wouldn't like to be the child," said Barbel   194   _____

disapprovingly. "Nobody knows anything about the old man up   203   _____

there. He never speaks to anybody. With his bushy eyebrows and   214   _____

terrible beard he looks a positive savage."   221   _____

Needs Work   1   2   3   4   5   Excellent
Paid attention to punctuation

Needs Work   1   2   3   4   5   Excellent
Sounded good

Total Words Read   _____

Total Errors   − _____

Correct WPM   _____

from *Heidi*

by Johanna Spyri

	Words Read	Miscues
Dete stood still. A stout, kind-looking woman came out of the	11	_____
house and joined them. "Where are you taking the child, Dete?"	22	_____
she asked. "I suppose it is your sister's child—the orphan?"	33	_____
"Yes," answered Dete. "I am taking her to stay with Alm-Uncle."	44	_____
"Surely you aren't going to leave the child with *him*. You must	56	_____
be out of your mind, Dete! But the old man is sure to turn you	71	_____
away, in any case!"	75	_____
"He can't do that! After all, he is her grandfather. I have looked	88	_____
after the child up till now, and I can tell you, Barbel, I am not	103	_____
going to turn down the offer of a good job on her account. From	117	_____
now on the grandfather will have to do his bit as well."	129	_____
"Oh, well, if he were like other people—" replied Barbel, "but	140	_____
you know him as well as I do. How can he look after a child, and	156	_____
especially such a little one? Oh, she will never stay with him! But	169	_____
where are *you* going, Dete?"	174	_____
"To a very good job in Frankfurt," explained Dete.	183	_____
"Well, I certainly wouldn't like to be the child," said Barbel	194	_____
disapprovingly. "Nobody knows anything about the old man up	203	_____
there. He never speaks to anybody. With his bushy eyebrows and	214	_____
terrible beard he looks a positive savage."	221	_____

Needs Work   1 2 3 4 5   Excellent
Paid attention to punctuation

Needs Work   1 2 3 4 5   Excellent
Sounded good

Total Words Read _____

Total Errors − _____

Correct WPM _____

27

Fiction

from *Shane*

by Jack Schaefer

First Reading

	Words Read	Miscues

Again and again they heaved at [the tree stump]. Each time it   12 _____
would angle up a bit farther. Each time it would fall back. They   25 _____
had it up once about a foot and a half, and that was the limit.   40 _____
They could not get past it.   46 _____

They stopped, breathing hard, mighty streaked now from the   55 _____
sweat rivulets down their faces. Father peered underneath as best   65 _____
he could. "Must be a taproot," he said. That was the one time   78 _____
either of them had spoken to the other, as far as I knew, the whole   93 _____
afternoon through. Father did not say anything more. And [the   103 _____
hired hand] Shane said nothing. He just picked up his axe and   115 _____
looked at father and waited.   120 _____

Father began to shake his head. There was some unspoken   130 _____
thought between them that bothered him. He looked down at his   141 _____
own big hands and slowly the fingers curled until they were   152 _____
clenched into big fists. Then his head stopped shaking and he   163 _____
stood taller and he drew a deep breath. He turned and backed in   176 _____
between two cut root ends, pressing against the stump. He pushed   187 _____
his feet into the ground for firm footholds. He bent his knees and   200 _____
slid his shoulders down the stump and wrapped his big hands   211 _____
around the root ends. Slowly he began to straighten. Slowly that   222 _____
huge old stump began to rise.   228 _____

Needs Work   1   2   3   4   5   Excellent
Paid attention to punctuation

Needs Work   1   2   3   4   5   Excellent
Sounded good

Total Words Read   _____

Total Errors − _____

Correct WPM   _____

from *Shane*

by Jack Schaefer

Again and again they heaved at [the tree stump]. Each time it	12	_____
would angle up a bit farther. Each time it would fall back. They	25	_____
had it up once about a foot and a half, and that was the limit.	40	_____
They could not get past it.	46	_____
They stopped, breathing hard, mighty streaked now from the	55	_____
sweat rivulets down their faces. Father peered underneath as best	65	_____
he could. "Must be a taproot," he said. That was the one time	78	_____
either of them had spoken to the other, as far as I knew, the whole	93	_____
afternoon through. Father did not say anything more. And [the	103	_____
hired hand] Shane said nothing. He just picked up his axe and	115	_____
looked at father and waited.	120	_____
Father began to shake his head. There was some unspoken	130	_____
thought between them that bothered him. He looked down at his	141	_____
own big hands and slowly the fingers curled until they were	152	_____
clenched into big fists. Then his head stopped shaking and he	163	_____
stood taller and he drew a deep breath. He turned and backed in	176	_____
between two cut root ends, pressing against the stump. He pushed	187	_____
his feet into the ground for firm footholds. He bent his knees and	200	_____
slid his shoulders down the stump and wrapped his big hands	211	_____
around the root ends. Slowly he began to straighten. Slowly that	222	_____
huge old stump began to rise.	228	_____

28
Fiction

from *Pirate's Promise*
by Clyde Robert Bulla

	Words Read	Miscues

There was only one room, and it was empty. — 9 _____

Benjy told Tom and the captain, "Do not go inside yet. There — 21 _____
may be snakes or spiders with poison in their bites." — 31 _____

He went into the house. With a palm branch he swept the — 43 _____
walls and floor. He put up the hammock and set the sea chest — 56 _____
beside it. — 58 _____

Afterward Tom went with him to find food and water. They — 69 _____
went to a clearing in the jungle. There was a well in the clearing. — 83 _____

Benjy took the cover off the well. He let down the bottle and — 96 _____
drew it up full of water. — 102 _____

Near the well Tom found a vine heavy with grapes. — 112 _____

"Pick some for our captain," said Benjy, "while I find — 122 _____
something more." — 124 _____

He took the pistol out of his belt. He went on into the jungle. — 138 _____

Tom put two leaves together to make a basket. He filled it with — 151 _____
grapes. Then he sat down on the well cover to wait for Benjy. — 164 _____

He thought of his sister, Dinah. He wondered how long it would — 176 _____
be before they were together again. How surprised she would be, — 187 _____
he thought, if she could see him here in this island jungle! — 199 _____

Needs Work 1 2 3 4 5 Excellent
Paid attention to punctuation

Needs Work 1 2 3 4 5 Excellent
Sounded good

Total Words Read _____

Total Errors − _____

Correct WPM _____

from *Pirate's Promise*
by Clyde Robert Bulla

	Words Read	Miscues
There was only one room, and it was empty.	9	_____
Benjy told Tom and the captain, "Do not go inside yet. There	21	_____
may be snakes or spiders with poison in their bites."	31	_____
He went into the house. With a palm branch he swept the	43	_____
walls and floor. He put up the hammock and set the sea chest	56	_____
beside it.	58	_____
Afterward Tom went with him to find food and water. They	69	_____
went to a clearing in the jungle. There was a well in the clearing.	83	_____
Benjy took the cover off the well. He let down the bottle and	96	_____
drew it up full of water.	102	_____
Near the well Tom found a vine heavy with grapes.	112	_____
"Pick some for our captain," said Benjy, "while I find	122	_____
something more."	124	_____
He took the pistol out of his belt. He went on into the jungle.	138	_____
Tom put two leaves together to make a basket. He filled it with	151	_____
grapes. Then he sat down on the well cover to wait for Benjy.	164	_____
He thought of his sister, Dinah. He wondered how long it would	176	_____
be before they were together again. How surprised she would be,	187	_____
he thought, if she could see him here in this island jungle!	199	_____

Needs Work   1   2   3   4   5   Excellent
Paid attention to punctuation

Needs Work   1   2   3   4   5   Excellent
Sounded good

Total Words Read   _____

Total Errors – _____

Correct WPM   _____

29

Fiction

from **"Splendor"**
by Lois Lowry

	Words Read	Miscues

To Becky's surprise, her mother smiled. "You have your baby- **10** _____
sitting money in the bank, Beck," she said. "And it's your very **21** _____
first real dance. If you want to spend that much on a special **34** _____
dress—well, it's up to you." **40** _____

"Mom," said Angela, "nobody dances with seventh graders **48** _____
anyway. The seventh-grade boys won't dance. They all stand **57** _____
around in the corners with each other. And the eighth-grade **67** _____
boys only dance with the eighth-grade girls. So what's the point **78** _____
of spending all your money on a dress if no one's going to dance **92** _____
with you? I *told* Becky she could wear my blue dress to the dance. **106** _____
The one I wore last year." **112** _____

"I don't want to wear a hand-me-down dress, not to the **123** _____
Christmas dance," Becky exploded. "*You* didn't have to wear **132** _____
someone else's dress when you were in seventh grade!" **141** _____

"Becky," Angela pointed out in her logical, patronizing way, **150** _____
"*I* didn't have an older sister. So who could hand a dress down?" **163** _____

"It's not my fault I was born second." **171** _____

"Shhh," said their mother. "Calm down. You buy the dress, **181** _____
honey, if it's what you want. It's important to have a very special **194** _____
dress now and then." **198** _____

Needs Work   1   2   3   4   5   Excellent
Paid attention to punctuation

Needs Work   1   2   3   4   5   Excellent
Sounded good

Total Words Read   _____

Total Errors   −   _____

Correct WPM   _____

from **"Splendor"**

by Lois Lowry

To Becky's surprise, her mother smiled. "You have your baby-	10 _____
sitting money in the bank, Beck," she said. "And it's your very	21 _____
first real dance. If you want to spend that much on a special	34 _____
dress—well, it's up to you."	40 _____
"Mom," said Angela, "nobody dances with seventh graders	48 _____
anyway. The seventh-grade boys won't dance. They all stand	57 _____
around in the corners with each other. And the eighth-grade	67 _____
boys only dance with the eighth-grade girls. So what's the point	78 _____
of spending all your money on a dress if no one's going to dance	92 _____
with you? I *told* Becky she could wear my blue dress to the dance.	106 _____
The one I wore last year."	112 _____
"I don't want to wear a hand-me-down dress, not to the	123 _____
Christmas dance," Becky exploded. "*You* didn't have to wear	132 _____
someone else's dress when you were in seventh grade!"	141 _____
"Becky," Angela pointed out in her logical, patronizing way,	150 _____
"*I* didn't have an older sister. So who could hand a dress down?"	163 _____
"It's not my fault I was born second."	171 _____
"Shhh," said their mother. "Calm down. You buy the dress,	181 _____
honey, if it's what you want. It's important to have a very special	194 _____
dress now and then."	198 _____

Needs Work   1   2   3   4   5   Excellent
            Paid attention to punctuation

Needs Work   1   2   3   4   5   Excellent
            Sounded good

Total Words Read   _____

Total Errors   −   _____

Correct WPM   _____

30

Fiction

from *The House on Mango Street*
by Sandra Cisneros

	Words Read	Miscues

There are stairs in our house, but they're ordinary hallway stairs, — 11

and the house has only one washroom. Everybody has to share — 22

a bedroom—Mama and Papa, Carlos and Kiki, me and Nenny. — 33

Once when we were living on Loomis, a nun from my school — 45

passed by and saw me playing out front. The laundromat — 55

downstairs had been boarded up because it had been robbed two — 66

days before and the owner had painted on the wood YES WE'RE — 78

OPEN so as not to lose business. — 85

Where do you live? she asked. — 91

There, I said pointing up to the third floor. — 100

You live *there?* — 103

There. I had to look to where she pointed—the third floor, the — 116

paint peeling, wooden bars Papa had nailed on the windows so — 127

we wouldn't fall out. You live *there?* The way she said it made me — 141

feel like nothing. *There.* I lived *there.* I nodded. — 150

I knew then I had to have a house. A real house. One I could — 165

point to. But this isn't it. The house on Mango Street isn't it. For — 179

the time being, Mama says. Temporary, says Papa. But I know — 190

how those things go. — 194

Needs Work   1   2   3   4   5   Excellent
        Paid attention to punctuation

Needs Work   1   2   3   4   5   Excellent
        Sounded good

Total Words Read _____

Total Errors − _____

Correct WPM _____

from *The House on Mango Street*
by Sandra Cisneros

	Words Read	Miscues
There are stairs in our house, but they're ordinary hallway stairs,	11	_____
and the house has only one washroom. Everybody has to share	22	_____
a bedroom—Mama and Papa, Carlos and Kiki, me and Nenny.	33	_____
Once when we were living on Loomis, a nun from my school	45	_____
passed by and saw me playing out front. The laundromat	55	_____
downstairs had been boarded up because it had been robbed two	66	_____
days before and the owner had painted on the wood YES WE'RE	78	_____
OPEN so as not to lose business.	85	_____
Where do you live? she asked.	91	_____
There, I said pointing up to the third floor.	100	_____
You live *there?*	103	_____
There. I had to look to where she pointed—the third floor, the	116	_____
paint peeling, wooden bars Papa had nailed on the windows so	127	_____
we wouldn't fall out. You live *there?* The way she said it made me	141	_____
feel like nothing. *There.* I lived *there.* I nodded.	150	_____
I knew then I had to have a house. A real house. One I could	165	_____
point to. But this isn't it. The house on Mango Street isn't it. For	179	_____
the time being, Mama says. Temporary, says Papa. But I know	190	_____
how those things go.	194	_____

Needs Work   1 2 3 4 5   Excellent
Paid attention to punctuation

Needs Work   1 2 3 4 5   Excellent
Sounded good

Total Words Read _____

Total Errors − _____

Correct WPM _____

31

Fiction

from *One-Eyed Cat*
by Paula Fox

	Words Read	Miscues

"Happy Birthday, Ned," his mother said. She was dressed | 9 | _____
and in her wheelchair. He could see from the door that she was | 22 | _____
holding something in her hands. "Come here to me," she said. | 33 | _____

Some mornings he walked to school and some mornings | 42 | _____
Papa drove him in the Packard. What was unvarying was that | 53 | _____
his mother's door was closed when he tiptoed past it, his school | 65 | _____
books under his arm, and went downstairs to his breakfast. He | 76 | _____
could not remember her ever having been up this early to wish | 88 | _____
him *Happy Birthday*. It meant that Papa had risen very early to do | 101 | _____
her hair and help her dress and carry her to the chair. He dropped | 115 | _____
his books on the bed as he went to her. He felt shy; he wasn't | 130 | _____
accustomed to seeing her at the start of his day. | 140 | _____

Her hands opened. On her palms lay a gold pocket watch | 151 | _____
nearly as flat as a wafer, its chain wound round her fingers like | 164 | _____
a golden grass snake. | 168 | _____

"This watch was my father's," she said. "Now it's yours." She | 179 | _____
lifted it up to him. He took it and held it to his ear. It ticked softly. | 196 | _____

Needs Work 1 2 3 4 5 Excellent
Paid attention to punctuation

Needs Work 1 2 3 4 5 Excellent
Sounded good

Total Words Read _____

Total Errors − _____

Correct WPM _____

from *One-Eyed Cat*
by Paula Fox

	Words Read	Miscues
"Happy Birthday, Ned," his mother said. She was dressed	9	_____
and in her wheelchair. He could see from the door that she was	22	_____
holding something in her hands. "Come here to me," she said.	33	_____
Some mornings he walked to school and some mornings	42	_____
Papa drove him in the Packard. What was unvarying was that	53	_____
his mother's door was closed when he tiptoed past it, his school	65	_____
books under his arm, and went downstairs to his breakfast. He	76	_____
could not remember her ever having been up this early to wish	88	_____
him *Happy Birthday.* It meant that Papa had risen very early to do	101	_____
her hair and help her dress and carry her to the chair. He dropped	115	_____
his books on the bed as he went to her. He felt shy; he wasn't	130	_____
accustomed to seeing her at the start of his day.	140	_____
Her hands opened. On her palms lay a gold pocket watch	151	_____
nearly as flat as a wafer, its chain wound round her fingers like	164	_____
a golden grass snake.	168	_____
"This watch was my father's," she said. "Now it's yours." She	179	_____
lifted it up to him. He took it and held it to his ear. It ticked softly.	196	_____

Needs Work 1 2 3 4 5 Excellent
Paid attention to punctuation

Needs Work 1 2 3 4 5 Excellent
Sounded good

Total Words Read _____

Total Errors − _____

Correct WPM _____

32
Fiction

from *Cave Under the City*
by Harry Mazer

	Words Read	Miscues
	First Reading	

I remembered the smell in the house when my mother seared   11   _____
the meat in the pot, then added onions and potatoes and carrots   23   _____
and stewed it slowly. And the good feeling of fat and meat in   36   _____
my belly.   38   _____

A woman in a dark coat came out of a store. "Carry your   51   _____
bundles, lady?"   53   _____

She pushed two heavy grocery bags into my arms and marched   64   _____
off. She lived three blocks from the store, on the second floor. By   77   _____
the time she unlocked the door, my arms felt like they were falling   90   _____
off. I set the bags down on the kitchen table. Something good was   103   _____
cooking. Everything in the apartment was clean and warm.   112   _____

She tied on an apron, looked at the bags on the table, and   125   _____
then gave me a dime. "Is that your little brother?" Bubber was just   138   _____
standing there. "You want a dime, too? Give me a smile," she said.   151   _____
He smiled at her. "What a sweet little boy." And she gave Bubber   164   _____
a dime, too.   167   _____

We bought a quart of milk and a box of sugar cookies and   180   _____
stood in an alleyway and ate everything.   187   _____

When it got dark we went home. A woman passed, carrying a   199   _____
fish wrapped in newspaper. "Go home, children," she sang. "Your   209   _____
mother is waiting for you."   214   _____

Needs Work   1 2 3 4 5   Excellent
Paid attention to punctuation

Needs Work   1 2 3 4 5   Excellent
Sounded good

Total Words Read _____

Total Errors − _____

Correct WPM _____

from *Cave Under the City*

by Harry Mazer

	Words Read	Miscues

I remembered the smell in the house when my mother seared	11	_____
the meat in the pot, then added onions and potatoes and carrots	23	_____
and stewed it slowly. And the good feeling of fat and meat in	36	_____
my belly.	38	_____
A woman in a dark coat came out of a store. "Carry your	51	_____
bundles, lady?"	53	_____
She pushed two heavy grocery bags into my arms and marched	64	_____
off. She lived three blocks from the store, on the second floor. By	77	_____
the time she unlocked the door, my arms felt like they were falling	90	_____
off. I set the bags down on the kitchen table. Something good was	103	_____
cooking. Everything in the apartment was clean and warm.	112	_____
She tied on an apron, looked at the bags on the table, and	125	_____
then gave me a dime. "Is that your little brother?" Bubber was just	138	_____
standing there. "You want a dime, too? Give me a smile," she said.	151	_____
He smiled at her. "What a sweet little boy." And she gave Bubber	164	_____
a dime, too.	167	_____
We bought a quart of milk and a box of sugar cookies and	180	_____
stood in an alleyway and ate everything.	187	_____
When it got dark we went home. A woman passed, carrying a	199	_____
fish wrapped in newspaper. "Go home, children," she sang. "Your	209	_____
mother is waiting for you."	214	_____

Needs Work   1 2 3 4 5 Excellent

Paid attention to punctuation

Needs Work   1 2 3 4 5 Excellent

Sounded good

Total Words Read _____

Total Errors −_____

Correct WPM _____

33

Fiction

from *Summer Hawk*
by Deborah Savage

	Words Read	Miscues

I followed [Rail] behind the trailer to the shed. Inside, he carefully — 12 _____

opened the sack in a large wire cage. He had to prod the hawk to — 27 _____

get her out. She half-skidded onto the floor of the cage, blinking, — 39 _____

and huddled in the corner without moving. She was still panting, — 50 _____

and her filthy down and feathers stuck out in every direction. — 61 _____

"She must be thirsty," I whispered. — 67 _____

"She gets water from meat," said Rail. "She wouldn't know how — 78 _____

to drink. I'll get a couple of squirrels this afternoon." — 88 _____

I didn't want to leave the hawk. I knelt and peered into the — 101 _____

cage, searching for some sign of her earlier defiance. But her eyes — 113 _____

were half-covered with a whitish lid and her head drooped. "Will — 124 _____

she be all right?" I asked. "When will she fly? When can we set — 138 _____

her free?" — 140 _____

Rail squatted next to me. "She's awful scared," he said pensively. — 151 _____

"But I'll fix her, Taylor. You'll see. She'll fly. You can tell she's a real — 166 _____

fighter." He brushed a cobweb off the wire mesh, but the hawk — 178 _____

didn't appear to notice. After a pause, Rail added, without looking — 189 _____

at me, "You can help. If you want, I mean. You can come over any — 204 _____

time you want." — 207 _____

Needs Work   1 2 3 4 5   Excellent
Paid attention to punctuation

Needs Work   1 2 3 4 5   Excellent
Sounded good

Total Words Read _____

Total Errors − _____

Correct WPM _____

from *Summer Hawk*
by Deborah Savage

I followed [Rail] behind the trailer to the shed. Inside, he carefully	12	_____
opened the sack in a large wire cage. He had to prod the hawk to	27	_____
get her out. She half-skidded onto the floor of the cage, blinking,	39	_____
and huddled in the corner without moving. She was still panting,	50	_____
and her filthy down and feathers stuck out in every direction.	61	_____
"She must be thirsty," I whispered.	67	_____
"She gets water from meat," said Rail. "She wouldn't know how	78	_____
to drink. I'll get a couple of squirrels this afternoon."	88	_____
I didn't want to leave the hawk. I knelt and peered into the	101	_____
cage, searching for some sign of her earlier defiance. But her eyes	113	_____
were half-covered with a whitish lid and her head drooped. "Will	124	_____
she be all right?" I asked. "When will she fly? When can we set	138	_____
her free?"	140	_____
Rail squatted next to me. "She's awful scared," he said pensively.	151	_____
"But I'll fix her, Taylor. You'll see. She'll fly. You can tell she's a real	166	_____
fighter." He brushed a cobweb off the wire mesh, but the hawk	178	_____
didn't appear to notice. After a pause, Rail added, without looking	189	_____
at me, "You can help. If you want, I mean. You can come over any	204	_____
time you want."	207	_____

Needs Work   1   2   3   4   5   Excellent
Paid attention to punctuation

Needs Work   1   2   3   4   5   Excellent
Sounded good

Total Words Read   _____

Total Errors − _____

Correct WPM   _____

34

Nonfiction

from *The Moon of the Bears*
by Jean Craighead George

First Reading

	Words Read	Miscues

A snowstorm blew down on the mountain, and the young bear   11 _____

became so sleepy that she stopped eating. Sitting on her haunches   22 _____

beside the log, she waited for the signal from the earth that   34 _____

would send her off to bed. Her head drooped, her chunky body   46 _____

rocked from side to side, and her big black feet curled up at the   60 _____

toes. She dozed and awoke, but she did not go into her den.   73 _____

One morning in November the air pressed down heavily upon   83 _____

her. The barometer was falling. The sky was dark, the valleys   94 _____

plunged in clouds. The wind whistled along the ridge, bringing   104 _____

snow. The flakes fell faster and faster. The bear sat by her den.   117 _____

The snow melted on her warm nose and fur. Still she did not go   131 _____

to bed. The temperature dropped into the teens. A wild, blustery   142 _____

wind picked up the snow and drove it against trees and rocks.   154 _____

With that the bear got to her feet. Head down, eyes squinting,   166 _____

she walked to her den and went in. With sweeps of her paws she   180 _____

tossed leaves and sticks over herself, then slumped to her haunches.   191 _____

A bluebottle fly, too cold to move, fell from the underside of the   204 _____

log onto her fur and sat still. The wind and snow swirled on.   217 _____

Needs Work   1   2   3   4   5   Excellent
_____
Paid attention to punctuation

Needs Work   1   2   3   4   5   Excellent
_____
Sounded good

Total Words Read   _____

Total Errors   − _____

Correct WPM   _____

from ***The Moon of the Bears***

by Jean Craighead George

A snowstorm blew down on the mountain, and the young bear	11	_____
became so sleepy that she stopped eating. Sitting on her haunches	22	_____
beside the log, she waited for the signal from the earth that	34	_____
would send her off to bed. Her head drooped, her chunky body	46	_____
rocked from side to side, and her big black feet curled up at the	60	_____
toes. She dozed and awoke, but she did not go into her den.	73	_____
One morning in November the air pressed down heavily upon	83	_____
her. The barometer was falling. The sky was dark, the valleys	94	_____
plunged in clouds. The wind whistled along the ridge, bringing	104	_____
snow. The flakes fell faster and faster. The bear sat by her den.	117	_____
The snow melted on her warm nose and fur. Still she did not go	131	_____
to bed. The temperature dropped into the teens. A wild, blustery	142	_____
wind picked up the snow and drove it against trees and rocks.	154	_____
With that the bear got to her feet. Head down, eyes squinting,	166	_____
she walked to her den and went in. With sweeps of her paws she	180	_____
tossed leaves and sticks over herself, then slumped to her haunches.	191	_____
A bluebottle fly, too cold to move, fell from the underside of the	204	_____
log onto her fur and sat still. The wind and snow swirled on.	217	_____

Needs Work   1 2 3 4 5   Excellent

Paid attention to punctuation

Needs Work   1 2 3 4 5   Excellent

Sounded good

Total Words Read _____

Total Errors − _____

Correct WPM _____

35

Nonfiction

from ***What's in the Deep?***

by Alese and Morton Pechter

	Words Read	Miscues

Another curious fish swam by.

"That's a scrawled filefish," said Todd. "He has black spots and beautiful blue markings on his body. As he swims along he can change his color from very pale to very bright."

"Why does he do that?" Patricia asked.

"He changes his color to blend in with the seascape," answered Todd. "That way he can search for food without being seen by his enemies."

"Do all fish play tricks with their colors?" Patricia asked Todd.

"Most of them do have some way of fooling bigger fish," Todd agreed. "This one here is a cowfish. He's covered by a hard shell. See the two 'horns' on top of his head? The horns make him hard to swallow, so the bigger fish pass him by when they're looking for a meal."

"Would the shark pass him up for something easier to swallow?" Patricia asked.

"Oh, no," Todd said. "When it comes to getting a meal, sharks aren't put off by anything. They've been known to take a bite out of an old tire or an oil drum."

The next fish they spotted was a white spotted trunkfish. His body was covered with a solid shell just like the cowfish.

Words Read
5
16
28
37
44
55
67
69
80
92
105
119
132
134
145
147
159
172
180
191
202

Needs Work 1 2 3 4 5 Excellent
Paid attention to punctuation

Needs Work 1 2 3 4 5 Excellent
Sounded good

Total Words Read _____

Total Errors – _____

Correct WPM _____

from ***What's in the Deep?***

by Alese and Morton Pechter

	Words Read	Miscues

Another curious fish swam by. — 5 _____

"That's a scrawled filefish," said Todd. "He has black spots and — 16 _____

beautiful blue markings on his body. As he swims along he can — 28 _____

change his color from very pale to very bright." — 37 _____

"Why does he do that?" Patricia asked. — 44 _____

"He changes his color to blend in with the seascape," answered — 55 _____

Todd. "That way he can search for food without being seen by — 67 _____

his enemies." — 69 _____

"Do all fish play tricks with their colors?" Patricia asked Todd. — 80 _____

"Most of them do have some way of fooling bigger fish," Todd — 92 _____

agreed. "This one here is a cowfish. He's covered by a hard shell. — 105 _____

See the two 'horns' on top of his head? The horns make him hard — 119 _____

to swallow, so the bigger fish pass him by when they're looking for — 132 _____

a meal." — 134 _____

"Would the shark pass him up for something easier to swallow?" — 145 _____

Patricia asked. — 147 _____

"Oh, no," Todd said. "When it comes to getting a meal, sharks — 159 _____

aren't put off by anything. They've been known to take a bite out — 172 _____

of an old tire or an oil drum." — 180 _____

The next fish they spotted was a white spotted trunkfish. His — 191 _____

body was covered with a solid shell just like the cowfish. — 202 _____

Needs Work   1   2   3   4   5   Excellent

Paid attention to punctuation

Needs Work   1   2   3   4   5   Excellent

Sounded good

Total Words Read _____

Total Errors − _____

Correct WPM _____

36

Fiction

from *I Sailed with Columbus*
by Miriam Schlein

First Reading

	Words Read	Miscues

When I awoke, the big square sail above was filled. At last we   13   _____

had some good wind. We should sail well today and make up for   26   _____

yesterday. But soon there was another problem. We were taking in   37   _____

too much water. The bilge (the lowest part of the hold) was filling,   50   _____

causing the *Santa María* to wallow and roll. Also, if water gets to   63   _____

our stores, they will rot. There is a pump down in the bilge, but it   78   _____

did not work fast enough. So every man not needed for the sailing   91   _____

of the ship (including me) was busy bailing. Buckets were filled in   103   _____

the bilge, passed along, dumped, then handed down again.   112   _____

It stank down in the bilge. We stood knee deep in water. Dead   125   _____

insects, and sometimes a rat, floated by. We took turns down there.   137   _____

No one could stay for long. In addition to the stink, the ship's   150   _____

rolling is worse down below.   155   _____

It was a long, wearying day. But at least I had the answer   168   _____

to my question: Did I get seasick? No. Only a little dizzy. Poor   181   _____

Diego, though, so eager to be a grown-up full seaman, had a   193   _____

terrible time.   195   _____

Needs Work   1   2   3   4   5   Excellent
Paid attention to punctuation

Needs Work   1   2   3   4   5   Excellent
Sounded good

Total Words Read   _____

Total Errors   – _____

Correct WPM   _____

from *I Sailed with Columbus*

by Miriam Schlein

When I awoke, the big square sail above was filled. At last we	13	_____
had some good wind. We should sail well today and make up for	26	_____
yesterday. But soon there was another problem. We were taking in	37	_____
too much water. The bilge (the lowest part of the hold) was filling,	50	_____
causing the *Santa María* to wallow and roll. Also, if water gets to	63	_____
our stores, they will rot. There is a pump down in the bilge, but it	78	_____
did not work fast enough. So every man not needed for the sailing	91	_____
of the ship (including me) was busy bailing. Buckets were filled in	103	_____
the bilge, passed along, dumped, then handed down again.	112	_____

It stank down in the bilge. We stood knee deep in water. Dead — 125
insects, and sometimes a rat, floated by. We took turns down there. — 137
No one could stay for long. In addition to the stink, the ship's — 150
rolling is worse down below. — 155

It was a long, wearying day. But at least I had the answer — 168
to my question: Did I get seasick? No. Only a little dizzy. Poor — 181
Diego, though, so eager to be a grown-up full seaman, had a — 193
terrible time. — 195

Needs Work   1   2   3   4   5   Excellent
Paid attention to punctuation

Needs Work   1   2   3   4   5   Excellent
Sounded good

Total Words Read _____

Total Errors − _____

Correct WPM _____

37 from *One Crowded Hour*
by Arthur Conan Doyle

Fiction

	Words Read	Miscues
"You're an early bird this morning," said Sir Henry as Ronald	11	_____
Barker walked toward him. "What's up? If you are going over	22	_____
to Lewes we could motor together."	28	_____
But Barker's demeanor was peculiar and ungracious. He	36	_____
disregarded the hand which was held out to him, and he stood	48	_____
staring with troubled, questioning eyes at the county magistrate.	57	_____
"Well, what's the matter?" asked the latter.	64	_____
Still the young man did not speak. He was clearly on the edge	77	_____
of an interview which he found it most difficult to open. His host	90	_____
grew impatient.	92	_____
"You don't seem yourself this morning. What on earth is the	103	_____
matter? Anything upset you?"	107	_____
"Yes," said Ronald Barker, with emphasis. "*You* have upset me."	117	_____
Sir Henry smiled. "Sit down, my dear fellow. If you have any	129	_____
grievance against me, let me hear it."	136	_____
Barker sat down. He seemed to be gathering himself for	146	_____
a reproach. When it did come it was like a bullet from a gun.	160	_____
"Why did you rob me last night?"	167	_____
The magistrate was a man of iron nerve. He showed neither	178	_____
surprise nor resentment. Not a muscle moved upon his calm,	188	_____
set face.	190	_____

Needs Work   1   2   3   4   5   Excellent
Paid attention to punctuation

Needs Work   1   2   3   4   5   Excellent
Sounded good

Total Words Read   _____

Total Errors − _____

Correct WPM   _____

from *One Crowded Hour*
by Arthur Conan Doyle

	Words Read	Miscues
"You're an early bird this morning," said Sir Henry as Ronald	11	_____
Barker walked toward him. "What's up? If you are going over	22	_____
to Lewes we could motor together."	28	_____
But Barker's demeanor was peculiar and ungracious. He	36	_____
disregarded the hand which was held out to him, and he stood	48	_____
staring with troubled, questioning eyes at the county magistrate.	57	_____
"Well, what's the matter?" asked the latter.	64	_____
Still the young man did not speak. He was clearly on the edge	77	_____
of an interview which he found it most difficult to open. His host	90	_____
grew impatient.	92	_____
"You don't seem yourself this morning. What on earth is the	103	_____
matter? Anything upset you?"	107	_____
"Yes," said Ronald Barker, with emphasis. "*You* have upset me."	117	_____
Sir Henry smiled. "Sit down, my dear fellow. If you have any	129	_____
grievance against me, let me hear it."	136	_____
Barker sat down. He seemed to be gathering himself for	146	_____
a reproach. When it did come it was like a bullet from a gun.	160	_____
"Why did you rob me last night?"	167	_____
The magistrate was a man of iron nerve. He showed neither	178	_____
surprise nor resentment. Not a muscle moved upon his calm,	188	_____
set face.	190	_____

Needs Work   1 2 3 4 5   Excellent
Paid attention to punctuation

Needs Work   1 2 3 4 5   Excellent
Sounded good

Total Words Read _____

Total Errors − _____

Correct WPM _____

38 Saving a Life

Nonfiction

Daniel Ortiz makes a common mistake. He jumps into the | 10 | _____

deep end of the town pool. He doesn't realize just how deep the | 23 | _____

water is. When he discovers that he can't touch the bottom of | 35 | _____

the pool, he panics. He tries to breathe, inhales water, and starts | 47 | _____

to sink. | 49 | _____

Lifeguard Bryant Kerns hears some splashing in the deep end | 59 | _____

of the pool and looks up. It could be nothing—kids playing—but | 72 | _____

Bryant's job is to make sure. To get a better look, he walks down | 86 | _____

to the deep end of the pool. There he sees Daniel Ortiz, sinking | 99 | _____

fast. Bryant yells for help. Then he dives in and swims toward | 111 | _____

Daniel. A pool employee quickly dials 911. | 118 | _____

Bryant reaches Daniel. Throwing an arm across Daniel's chest, | 127 | _____

Bryant pulls him to the side of the pool. Other hands help pull | 140 | _____

Daniel from the water. He's not breathing. Bryant starts CPR. | 150 | _____

Almost immediately, Daniel starts coughing. He throws up water | 159 | _____

and begins to gasp. | 163 | _____

By the time the ambulance arrives, Daniel is sitting up. His | 174 | _____

lungs sound clear, but the medics take him to the hospital just | 186 | _____

to be sure. | 189 | _____

As for Bryant, he denies that he's a hero. "I didn't have time | 202 | _____

to think," he says. "I just did what I'm trained to do. It's my job." | 217 | _____

Needs Work 1 2 3 4 5 Excellent
Paid attention to punctuation

Needs Work 1 2 3 4 5 Excellent
Sounded good

Total Words Read _____

Total Errors – _____

Correct WPM _____

Saving a Life

	Words Read	Miscues

Daniel Ortiz makes a common mistake. He jumps into the — 10

deep end of the town pool. He doesn't realize just how deep the — 23

water is. When he discovers that he can't touch the bottom of — 35

the pool, he panics. He tries to breathe, inhales water, and starts — 47

to sink. — 49

Lifeguard Bryant Kerns hears some splashing in the deep end — 59

of the pool and looks up. It could be nothing—kids playing—but — 72

Bryant's job is to make sure. To get a better look, he walks down — 86

to the deep end of the pool. There he sees Daniel Ortiz, sinking — 99

fast. Bryant yells for help. Then he dives in and swims toward — 111

Daniel. A pool employee quickly dials 911. — 118

Bryant reaches Daniel. Throwing an arm across Daniel's chest, — 127

Bryant pulls him to the side of the pool. Other hands help pull — 140

Daniel from the water. He's not breathing. Bryant starts CPR. — 150

Almost immediately, Daniel starts coughing. He throws up water — 159

and begins to gasp. — 163

By the time the ambulance arrives, Daniel is sitting up. His — 174

lungs sound clear, but the medics take him to the hospital just — 186

to be sure. — 189

As for Bryant, he denies that he's a hero. "I didn't have time — 202

to think," he says. "I just did what I'm trained to do. It's my job." — 217

Needs Work 1 2 3 4 5 Excellent
Paid attention to punctuation

Needs Work 1 2 3 4 5 Excellent
Sounded good

Total Words Read _____

Total Errors − _____

Correct WPM _____

39

Fiction

from *Shoeshine Girl*
by Clyde Robert Bulla

	Words Read	Miscues

Aunt Claudia smiled a little. "Here's the way I understand it.   11   _____

Your father's work takes him away from home a lot. You and   23   _____

your mother have had a few problems. Your mother isn't well—"   34   _____

     "That's what she says," said Sarah Ida.   41   _____

     "Your mother isn't well," Aunt Claudia said again, "and you   51   _____

weren't making things easy for her. She and your father thought   62   _____

it would be better if you came here for a while."   73   _____

     "That's their story," said Sarah Ida.   79   _____

     "Do you want to tell yours?"   85   _____

     "Not especially. I don't think you'd listen."   92   _____

     "You could try and see."   97   _____

     "Well—" Sarah Ida began. "For a long time nobody cared what   108   _____

I did. Nobody paid any attention. Then all at once everything   119   _____

changed. Mother asked a million questions about everything I   128   _____

did. And my clothes weren't right, and my friends weren't right.   139   _____

I couldn't do this—I couldn't do that."   147   _____

     "You say everything changed all at once," said Aunt Claudia.   157   _____

"Why was that?"   160   _____

     Sarah Ida looked away.   164   _____

     "You had a friend named Midge, didn't you?" said Aunt   174   _____

Claudia. "And Midge got into trouble. The way I heard it, she was   187   _____

taking a dress out of a store. It was a dress she hadn't paid for."   202   _____

     "She wasn't stealing," said Sarah Ida.   208   _____

     "What do you call it?" asked Aunt Claudia.   216   _____

Needs Work   1   2   3   4   5   Excellent
Paid attention to punctuation

Needs Work   1   2   3   4   5   Excellent
Sounded good

Total Words Read   _____

Total Errors   – _____

Correct WPM   _____

from *Shoeshine Girl*
by Clyde Robert Bulla

	Words Read	Miscues
Aunt Claudia smiled a little. "Here's the way I understand it.	11	_____
Your father's work takes him away from home a lot. You and	23	_____
your mother have had a few problems. Your mother isn't well—"	34	_____
"That's what she says," said Sarah Ida.	41	_____
"Your mother isn't well," Aunt Claudia said again, "and you	51	_____
weren't making things easy for her. She and your father thought	62	_____
it would be better if you came here for a while."	73	_____
"That's their story," said Sarah Ida.	79	_____
"Do you want to tell yours?"	85	_____
"Not especially. I don't think you'd listen."	92	_____
"You could try and see."	97	_____
"Well—" Sarah Ida began. "For a long time nobody cared what	108	_____
I did. Nobody paid any attention. Then all at once everything	119	_____
changed. Mother asked a million questions about everything I	128	_____
did. And my clothes weren't right, and my friends weren't right.	139	_____
I couldn't do this—I couldn't do that."	147	_____
"You say everything changed all at once," said Aunt Claudia.	157	_____
"Why was that?"	160	_____
Sarah Ida looked away.	164	_____
"You had a friend named Midge, didn't you?" said Aunt	174	_____
Claudia. "And Midge got into trouble. The way I heard it, she was	187	_____
taking a dress out of a store. It was a dress she hadn't paid for."	202	_____
"She wasn't stealing," said Sarah Ida.	208	_____
"What do you call it?" asked Aunt Claudia.	216	_____

Needs Work 1 2 3 4 5 **Excellent**
Paid attention to punctuation

Needs Work 1 2 3 4 5 **Excellent**
Sounded good

Total Words Read _____

Total Errors − _____

Correct WPM _____

40
Nonfiction

from *A Grain of Wheat:*
A Writer Begins
by Clyde Robert Bulla

	Words Read	Miscues

Our front porch faced west. I could sit there and see the barn | 13 | _____
lot with the big barn and small sheds. I could see the pasture and | 27 | _____
the woods. Beyond the woods I could see Will Sutton's little | 38 | _____
brown house half a mile away. | 44 | _____

My dog Carlo would be with me on the porch. He was a collie. | 58 | _____
He was the family dog before I was born, but as soon as I was old | 74 | _____
enough to play outside he became my dog. | 82 | _____

Most of our storms came out of the west. I liked to sit on the | 97 | _____
porch and watch them. The sky would turn dark, almost black. | 108 | _____
Lightning would split the clouds, and thunder would crash. Wind | 118 | _____
would blow and bend the trees, and I would see the rain like a | 132 | _____
gray curtain falling over the woods. It would sweep across the | 143 | _____
barn lot and onto the porch, onto my dog and me. | 154 | _____

Carlo was afraid of storms. He would shiver and push against | 165 | _____
me. I remember the smell of his wet fur. I would put my arms | 179 | _____
around him and we would sit there until my mother opened the | 191 | _____
door and found us. | 195 | _____

"You'll be *soaked*!" she would say and drag me into the | 206 | _____
kitchen. But Carlo would have to stay outside. | 214 | _____

Needs Work 1 2 3 4 5 Excellent
Paid attention to punctuation

Needs Work 1 2 3 4 5 Excellent
Sounded good

Total Words Read _____

Total Errors − _____

Correct WPM _____

from *A Grain of Wheat:*
A Writer Begins
by Clyde Robert Bulla

Second Reading

	Words Read	Miscues

⊛⊛⊛

Our front porch faced west. I could sit there and see the barn | 13 | _____
lot with the big barn and small sheds. I could see the pasture and | 27 | _____
the woods. Beyond the woods I could see Will Sutton's little | 38 | _____
brown house half a mile away. | 44 | _____

My dog Carlo would be with me on the porch. He was a collie. | 58 | _____
He was the family dog before I was born, but as soon as I was old | 74 | _____
enough to play outside he became my dog. | 82 | _____

Most of our storms came out of the west. I liked to sit on the | 97 | _____
porch and watch them. The sky would turn dark, almost black. | 108 | _____
Lightning would split the clouds, and thunder would crash. Wind | 118 | _____
would blow and bend the trees, and I would see the rain like a | 132 | _____
gray curtain falling over the woods. It would sweep across the | 143 | _____
barn lot and onto the porch, onto my dog and me. | 154 | _____

Carlo was afraid of storms. He would shiver and push against | 165 | _____
me. I remember the smell of his wet fur. I would put my arms | 179 | _____
around him and we would sit there until my mother opened the | 191 | _____
door and found us. | 195 | _____

"You'll be *soaked*!" she would say and drag me into the | 206 | _____
kitchen. But Carlo would have to stay outside. | 214 | _____

Needs Work   1   2   3   4   5   Excellent
Paid attention to punctuation

Needs Work   1   2   3   4   5   Excellent
Sounded good

Total Words Read _____

Total Errors − _____

Correct WPM _____

41

Nonfiction

George Gershwin:
An American Story

First Reading

	Words Read	Miscues

George Gershwin was born in 1898 in New York City. His   **11** _____
parents were new to America. They had come from Russia,   **21** _____
seeking a better life.   **25** _____

During George's childhood, his father had hopes for great   **34** _____
business success. He changed jobs often. Each time he changed   **44** _____
jobs, he moved his family. By the time George grew up, he   **56** _____
had moved more than twenty times.   **62** _____

George was not a scholar. He didn't like school. But he was   **74** _____
drawn to music. When he was twelve, his family bought a piano.   **86** _____
The hope was that his brother, Ira, would learn to play. Ira just   **99** _____
wasn't interested. But George would plink the keys every time he   **110** _____
passed by. He began taking lessons. Soon he was ready for a new   **123** _____
teacher. And then another.   **127** _____

At fifteen, he told his mother that he was ready to quit school   **140** _____
and go to work. He planned to make a living with music. His   **153** _____
mother was disappointed. She had her own hopes and dreams   **163** _____
for his life. But she did not stand in his way.   **174** _____

George got a job in Tin Pan Alley. He worked for a music   **187** _____
publisher. His job was to play the company's music for interested   **198** _____
buyers. It wasn't long before he grew bored with playing the same   **210** _____
songs. He began to add his own flourishes. People would gather   **221** _____
at his piano to hear him play.   **228** _____

Needs Work   1 2 3 4 5   Excellent
Paid attention to punctuation

Needs Work   1 2 3 4 5   Excellent
Sounded good

Total Words Read _____

Total Errors − _____

Correct WPM _____

George Gershwin:
An American Story

	Words Read	Miscues

George Gershwin was born in 1898 in New York City. His — 11 — _____
parents were new to America. They had come from Russia, — 21 — _____
seeking a better life. — 25 — _____

During George's childhood, his father had hopes for great — 34 — _____
business success. He changed jobs often. Each time he changed — 44 — _____
jobs, he moved his family. By the time George grew up, he — 56 — _____
had moved more than twenty times. — 62 — _____

George was not a scholar. He didn't like school. But he was — 74 — _____
drawn to music. When he was twelve, his family bought a piano. — 86 — _____
The hope was that his brother, Ira, would learn to play. Ira just — 99 — _____
wasn't interested. But George would plink the keys every time he — 110 — _____
passed by. He began taking lessons. Soon he was ready for a new — 123 — _____
teacher. And then another. — 127 — _____

At fifteen, he told his mother that he was ready to quit school — 140 — _____
and go to work. He planned to make a living with music. His — 153 — _____
mother was disappointed. She had her own hopes and dreams — 163 — _____
for his life. But she did not stand in his way. — 174 — _____

George got a job in Tin Pan Alley. He worked for a music — 187 — _____
publisher. His job was to play the company's music for interested — 198 — _____
buyers. It wasn't long before he grew bored with playing the same — 210 — _____
songs. He began to add his own flourishes. People would gather — 221 — _____
at his piano to hear him play. — 228 — _____

Needs Work 1 2 3 4 5 Excellent
Paid attention to punctuation

Needs Work 1 2 3 4 5 Excellent
Sounded good

Total Words Read _____

Total Errors − _____

Correct WPM _____

42
Nonfiction

from *The Big Sea*
by Langston Hughes

	Words Read	Miscues

    My two years in Washington were unhappy years, except **9** _____

for poetry and the friends I made through poetry. I wrote many **21** _____

poems. I always put them away new for several weeks in a bottom **34** _____

drawer. Then I would take them out and re-read them. If they **46** _____

seemed bad, I would throw them away. They would all seem good **58** _____

when I wrote them and, usually, bad when I would look at them **71** _____

again. So most of them were thrown away. **79** _____

    The blues poems I would often make up in my head and sing **92** _____

on the way to work. (Except that I could never carry a tune. But **106** _____

when I sing to myself, I think I am singing.) One evening, I was **120** _____

crossing Rock Creek Bridge, singing a blues I was trying to get **132** _____

right before I put it down on paper. A man passing on the **145** _____

opposite side of the bridge stopped, looked at me, then turned **156** _____

around and cut across the roadway. **162** _____

    He said: "Son, what's the matter? Are you ill?" **171** _____

    "No," I said. "Just singing." **176** _____

    "I thought you were groaning," he commented. "Sorry!" And **185** _____

went on his way. **189** _____

    So after that I never sang my verses aloud in the street any more. **203** _____

Needs Work   1   2   3   4   5   Excellent
Paid attention to punctuation

Needs Work   1   2   3   4   5   Excellent
Sounded good

Total Words Read   _____

Total Errors   – _____

Correct WPM   _____

42

Nonfiction

from *The Big Sea*

by Langston Hughes

	Words Read	Miscues

My two years in Washington were unhappy years, except   9   _____

for poetry and the friends I made through poetry. I wrote many   21   _____

poems. I always put them away new for several weeks in a bottom   34   _____

drawer. Then I would take them out and re-read them. If they   46   _____

seemed bad, I would throw them away. They would all seem good   58   _____

when I wrote them and, usually, bad when I would look at them   71   _____

again. So most of them were thrown away.   79   _____

     The blues poems I would often make up in my head and sing   92   _____

on the way to work. (Except that I could never carry a tune. But   106   _____

when I sing to myself, I think I am singing.) One evening, I was   120   _____

crossing Rock Creek Bridge, singing a blues I was trying to get   132   _____

right before I put it down on paper. A man passing on the   145   _____

opposite side of the bridge stopped, looked at me, then turned   156   _____

around and cut across the roadway.   162   _____

     He said: "Son, what's the matter? Are you ill?"   171   _____

     "No," I said. "Just singing."   176   _____

     "I thought you were groaning," he commented. "Sorry!" And   185   _____

went on his way.   189   _____

     So after that I never sang my verses aloud in the street any more.   203   _____

Needs Work   1   2   3   4   5   Excellent
     Paid attention to punctuation

Needs Work   1   2   3   4   5   Excellent
     Sounded good

Total Words Read   _____

Total Errors   − _____

Correct WPM   _____

43 Famine in Ireland

Fiction

First Reading

	Words Read	Miscues

Patrick O'Riordan looked with horror at his potato field. The   10 _____

leaves and stalks of the plants were black and slimy with fungus.   22 _____

The dreaded potato blight had arrived. Behind him he heard his   33 _____

wife cry, "Oh, no, Patrick! Whatever shall we do?"   42 _____

Do? There was nothing that could be done. There would be   53 _____

no potato crop this year. There would be no money to pay the   66 _____

landlord's rent. There would be no potatoes—their family's main   76 _____

source of food—to keep them fed through the winter. "We'll try   88 _____

to stay alive, Brigid," Patrick told her. "That's what we will do."   100 _____

That winter of 1846–47 was unusually severe. Patrick, Brigid,   109 _____

and their children huddled against the cold in their windowless   119 _____

mud hut. Brigid wrapped rags around her children's bare feet to   130 _____

protect them from the frozen ground. She stirred a pot of "soup"   142 _____

that hung over the fire—a soup of water, tree bark, and roots. It   156 _____

filled their stomachs but gave little nourishment. All of them grew   167 _____

thin and gaunt.   170 _____

Then the landlord's agent came. "You haven't paid the rent," he   181 _____

told them. "You have to leave." The O'Riordans gathered up their   192 _____

few possessions and left their home.   198 _____

"We'll go to America, Brigid," Patrick told her. "We'll start a   209 _____

new life there."   212 _____

Needs Work   1 2 3 4 5   Excellent
Paid attention to punctuation

Needs Work   1 2 3 4 5   Excellent
Sounded good

Total Words Read   _____

Total Errors   − _____

Correct WPM   _____

Famine in Ireland

Patrick O'Riordan looked with horror at his potato field. The	10	_____
leaves and stalks of the plants were black and slimy with fungus.	22	_____
The dreaded potato blight had arrived. Behind him he heard his	33	_____
wife cry, "Oh, no, Patrick! Whatever shall we do?"	42	_____
Do? There was nothing that could be done. There would be	53	_____
no potato crop this year. There would be no money to pay the	66	_____
landlord's rent. There would be no potatoes—their family's main	76	_____
source of food—to keep them fed through the winter. "We'll try	88	_____
to stay alive, Brigid," Patrick told her. "That's what we will do."	100	_____
That winter of 1846–47 was unusually severe. Patrick, Brigid,	109	_____
and their children huddled against the cold in their windowless	119	_____
mud hut. Brigid wrapped rags around her children's bare feet to	130	_____
protect them from the frozen ground. She stirred a pot of "soup"	142	_____
that hung over the fire—a soup of water, tree bark, and roots. It	156	_____
filled their stomachs but gave little nourishment. All of them grew	167	_____
thin and gaunt.	170	_____
Then the landlord's agent came. "You haven't paid the rent," he	181	_____
told them. "You have to leave." The O'Riordans gathered up their	192	_____
few possessions and left their home.	198	_____
"We'll go to America, Brigid," Patrick told her. "We'll start a	209	_____
new life there."	212	_____

Needs Work   1   2   3   4   5   Excellent
Paid attention to punctuation

Needs Work   1   2   3   4   5   Excellent
Sounded good

Total Words Read   _____

Total Errors   − _____

Correct WPM   _____

44 George Catlin:
Artist and Historian

Nonfiction

First Reading

	Words Read	Miscues

George Catlin was born in 1796. When he reached his teen | 11 | _____ |
years, his father chose a career for him—the law. George wanted | 23 | _____ |
to please his father. He tried the law. But in the back of his mind, | 38 | _____ |
his own dreams wouldn't rest. He loved to draw. Could he make | 50 | _____ |
a living with drawing? | 54 | _____ |

As time went by, George set up a studio in Philadelphia. There, | 66 | _____ |
he painted portraits for those who lived in the town. At first this | 79 | _____ |
work pleased him. But as his skills increased, he grew restless. He | 91 | _____ |
hungered to do more with his life. | 98 | _____ |

One day a group of Plains Indians passed through the town. | 109 | _____ |
The men wore buffalo robes and other traditional clothing. | 118 | _____ |
George was intrigued. He thought about the men and their way of | 130 | _____ |
life. He tried to picture them on their land and among their people. | 143 | _____ |

In his heart, he formed a goal. He would learn all he could | 156 | _____ |
about Native American people and the West. He would visit the | 167 | _____ |
different tribes on their own lands. He would paint key figures | 178 | _____ |
in the tribes. Through his paintings, he would capture the looks, | 189 | _____ |
dress, customs, and bearing of many Native American people. He | 199 | _____ |
wrote, "Nothing short of the loss of my life shall prevent me from | 212 | _____ |
visiting their country and becoming their historian." | 219 | _____ |

By 1830, George began to make good on his plan. | 229 | _____ |

Needs Work   1   2   3   4   5   Excellent
Paid attention to punctuation

Needs Work   1   2   3   4   5   Excellent
Sounded good

Total Words Read   _____

Total Errors   – _____

Correct WPM   _____

George Catlin:
Artist and Historian

	Words Read	Miscues
George Catlin was born in 1796. When he reached his teen	11	_____
years, his father chose a career for him—the law. George wanted	23	_____
to please his father. He tried the law. But in the back of his mind,	38	_____
his own dreams wouldn't rest. He loved to draw. Could he make	50	_____
a living with drawing?	54	_____
As time went by, George set up a studio in Philadelphia. There,	66	_____
he painted portraits for those who lived in the town. At first this	79	_____
work pleased him. But as his skills increased, he grew restless. He	91	_____
hungered to do more with his life.	98	_____
One day a group of Plains Indians passed through the town.	109	_____
The men wore buffalo robes and other traditional clothing.	118	_____
George was intrigued. He thought about the men and their way of	130	_____
life. He tried to picture them on their land and among their people.	143	_____
In his heart, he formed a goal. He would learn all he could	156	_____
about Native American people and the West. He would visit the	167	_____
different tribes on their own lands. He would paint key figures	178	_____
in the tribes. Through his paintings, he would capture the looks,	189	_____
dress, customs, and bearing of many Native American people. He	199	_____
wrote, "Nothing short of the loss of my life shall prevent me from	212	_____
visiting their country and becoming their historian."	219	_____
By 1830, George began to make good on his plan.	229	_____

Needs Work   1   2   3   4   5   Excellent

Paid attention to punctuation

Needs Work   1   2   3   4   5   Excellent

Sounded good

Total Words Read   _____

Total Errors   − _____

Correct WPM   _____

45
Fiction

from *It's Not the End of the World*
by Judy Blume

	Words Read	Miscues

As soon as we finished eating, my father and Jeff went outside to | 13 | _____

shovel the walk. Me and Amy were dying to go out too. Finally | 26 | _____

Mom said, "Okay . . . if you bundle up good and promise to come | 38 | _____

inside when you get cold." | 43 | _____

I helped Amy get ready. She has trouble with her boots. I tied | 56 | _____

up her hood and found her a pair of mittens. Then we went | 69 | _____

out together. | 71 | _____

When Jeff saw us he called, "How about a snowball fight? | 82 | _____

Me and Amy against Karen and Dad." | 89 | _____

"Okay," we called. | 92 | _____

Daddy and I hurried around to the side of our house and I | 105 | _____

made the snowballs for him to throw. Jeff and Amy hid behind | 117 | _____

the big tree and pretty soon the snow was flying. I think Daddy | 130 | _____

and I won but it didn't matter because it was such fun. When | 143 | _____

we got tired of throwing snowballs Amy and me lay down in the | 156 | _____

snow and made angels. I was moving my arms back and forth to | 169 | _____

make really good wings. Then I looked up at the sky. There were | 182 | _____

a million stars. I wanted everything to stay just the way it was— | 195 | _____

still and beautiful. | 198 | _____

Needs Work   1   2   3   4   5   Excellent
_____
Paid attention to punctuation

Needs Work   1   2   3   4   5   Excellent
_____
Sounded good

Total Words Read _____

Total Errors − _____

Correct WPM _____

from *It's Not the End of the World*
by Judy Blume

	Words Read	Miscues
As soon as we finished eating, my father and Jeff went outside to	13	_____
shovel the walk. Me and Amy were dying to go out too. Finally	26	_____
Mom said, "Okay . . . if you bundle up good and promise to come	38	_____
inside when you get cold."	43	_____
I helped Amy get ready. She has trouble with her boots. I tied	56	_____
up her hood and found her a pair of mittens. Then we went	69	_____
out together.	71	_____
When Jeff saw us he called, "How about a snowball fight?	82	_____
Me and Amy against Karen and Dad."	89	_____
"Okay," we called.	92	_____
Daddy and I hurried around to the side of our house and I	105	_____
made the snowballs for him to throw. Jeff and Amy hid behind	117	_____
the big tree and pretty soon the snow was flying. I think Daddy	130	_____
and I won but it didn't matter because it was such fun. When	143	_____
we got tired of throwing snowballs Amy and me lay down in the	156	_____
snow and made angels. I was moving my arms back and forth to	169	_____
make really good wings. Then I looked up at the sky. There were	182	_____
a million stars. I wanted everything to stay just the way it was—	195	_____
still and beautiful.	198	_____

Needs Work   1 2 3 4 5   Excellent
Paid attention to punctuation

Needs Work   1 2 3 4 5   Excellent
Sounded good

Total Words Read _____

Total Errors − _____

Correct WPM _____

46

Fiction

from *The Hundred Penny Box*

by Sharon Bell Mathis

First Reading

	Words Read	Miscues

"I mean," Michael said and tried to think fast. "Aunt Dew 　　11　　_____

won't go to sleep if she doesn't see her [penny] box in the corner. 　25　_____

Can I take it back and then you can let her see it? And when she 　41　_____

goes to sleep, you can take it." 　48　_____

"Go put it back in her room then," his mother said. "I'll get 　61　_____

it later." 　63　_____

"Okay," Michael said and held the heavy box tighter and walked 　74　_____

slowly back down the hall to the small bedroom that used to be 　87　_____

his. He opened the door and went in, put the hundred penny box 　100　_____

down on the floor and sat down on it, staring at his aunt. She 　114　_____

wasn't singing, just sitting. "John-boy," she said. 　121　_____

"Yes, Aunt Dew," Michael answered and didn't care this time 　131　_____

that she was calling him John again. He was trying to think. 　143　_____

"Put my music on." 　147　_____

The music wasn't going to help him think because the first 　158　_____

thing she was going to do was to make him "move" too. 　170　_____

But Michael got off the hundred penny box and reached 　180　_____

under his bed and pulled out his blue record player that he 　192　_____

had got for his birthday. 　197　_____

Needs Work　1　2　3　4　5　Excellent
Paid attention to punctuation

Needs Work　1　2　3　4　5　Excellent
Sounded good

Total Words Read _____

Total Errors − _____

Correct WPM _____

from *The Hundred Penny Box*
by Sharon Bell Mathis

	Words Read	Miscues

"I mean," Michael said and tried to think fast. "Aunt Dew · 11 · _____

won't go to sleep if she doesn't see her [penny] box in the corner. · 25 · _____

Can I take it back and then you can let her see it? And when she · 41 · _____

goes to sleep, you can take it." · 48 · _____

"Go put it back in her room then," his mother said. "I'll get · 61 · _____

it later." · 63 · _____

"Okay," Michael said and held the heavy box tighter and walked · 74 · _____

slowly back down the hall to the small bedroom that used to be · 87 · _____

his. He opened the door and went in, put the hundred penny box · 100 · _____

down on the floor and sat down on it, staring at his aunt. She · 114 · _____

wasn't singing, just sitting. "John-boy," she said. · 121 · _____

"Yes, Aunt Dew," Michael answered and didn't care this time · 131 · _____

that she was calling him John again. He was trying to think. · 143 · _____

"Put my music on." · 147 · _____

The music wasn't going to help him think because the first · 158 · _____

thing she was going to do was to make him "move" too. · 170 · _____

But Michael got off the hundred penny box and reached · 180 · _____

under his bed and pulled out his blue record player that he · 192 · _____

had got for his birthday. · 197 · _____

Needs Work   1   2   3   4   5   Excellent
Paid attention to punctuation

Needs Work   1   2   3   4   5   Excellent
Sounded good

Total Words Read _____

Total Errors − _____

Correct WPM _____

47 Fiction

from *Bandit's Moon*
by Sid Fleischman

I noticed four or five men standing around the no–name buckskin	11
I had tied outside the barbershop.	17
"That pony is stolen!" I heard a tall man shout. "It looks like	30
my nephew's long-haired buckskin down in Santa Barbara. I'd	39
know it anywhere! Look at the brand!"	46
Everyone clustered around to look at the brand. The barber	56
had come out to see what all the fuss was about. "Maybe there's	69
a cross brand," he said. "Your nephew might have sold the horse."	81
I found myself backing into a doorway; it turned out to be	93
the doorway of the sheriff's office. I should have had better sense	105
than to ride the buckskin into town. It didn't surprise me that	117
someone recognized the horse. It was just the sort of evil luck	129
that had my name all over it.	136
The men checked the left shoulder of the buckskin. There was	147
no second brand, as I guessed there would have been if the horse	160
had been sold fair and square.	166
"It's stolen, sure as a goose goes barefoot!"	174
"That's a hangin' crime! Anybody seen who rode the horse and	185
tied it up?"	188
The barber cleared his voice. "It was a skinny boy with turned-	200
up boots."	201

Needs Work   1   2   3   4   5   Excellent
Paid attention to punctuation

Needs Work   1   2   3   4   5   Excellent
Sounded good

Total Words Read _____

Total Errors – _____

Correct WPM _____

from *Bandit's Moon*

by Sid Fleischman

I noticed four or five men standing around the no-name buckskin | 11 | _____
I had tied outside the barbershop. | 17 | _____

"That pony is stolen!" I heard a tall man shout. "It looks like | 30 | _____
my nephew's long-haired buckskin down in Santa Barbara. I'd | 39 | _____
know it anywhere! Look at the brand!" | 46 | _____

Everyone clustered around to look at the brand. The barber | 56 | _____
had come out to see what all the fuss was about. "Maybe there's | 69 | _____
a cross brand," he said. "Your nephew might have sold the horse." | 81 | _____

I found myself backing into a doorway; it turned out to be | 93 | _____
the doorway of the sheriff's office. I should have had better sense | 105 | _____
than to ride the buckskin into town. It didn't surprise me that | 117 | _____
someone recognized the horse. It was just the sort of evil luck | 129 | _____
that had my name all over it. | 136 | _____

The men checked the left shoulder of the buckskin. There was | 147 | _____
no second brand, as I guessed there would have been if the horse | 160 | _____
had been sold fair and square. | 166 | _____

"It's stolen, sure as a goose goes barefoot!" | 174 | _____

"That's a hangin' crime! Anybody seen who rode the horse and | 185 | _____
tied it up?" | 188 | _____

The barber cleared his voice. "It was a skinny boy with turned- | 200 | _____
up boots." | 201 | _____

Needs Work   1   2   3   4   5   Excellent
Paid attention to punctuation

Needs Work   1   2   3   4   5   Excellent
Sounded good

Total Words Read _____

Total Errors − _____

Correct WPM _____

48
Nonfiction

from *Buffalo Bill:*
Wild West Showman
by Mary R. Davidson

First Reading

	Words Read	Miscues

Once a large sum of money was to be sent in the mail [via the   15 _____

Pony Express]. The company asked for volunteers. Some robbers   24 _____

had already killed one rider they thought had the money.   34 _____

Bill Cody offered to take the money through. He was held   45 _____

up by one gang. But he escaped on his fast pony. Later, two men   59 _____

stopped him with six-shooters.   63 _____

"We know you, Bill," one of them said. "We know you've got   75 _____

the money. Hand over that pouch."   81 _____

Bill had two pouches with him. He had filled one pouch with   93 _____

waste paper. He threw this pouch hard at one of the men and shot   107 _____

him in the arm. Then he ran his horse into the second robber.   120 _____

Before the first man could shoot, Bill was well on his way.   132 _____

He carried the money through to his station. He rode over three   144 _____

hundred miles without stopping to rest.   150 _____

The work was hard, too hard for a fifteen-year-old. Night   160 _____

after night, Bill fell into bed, too tired to take off his clothes.   173 _____

The Pony Express was very famous. But it lasted only a few   185 _____

months. Soon there was no need for it. Telegraph poles were   196 _____

springing up all through the West. Telegraph wires could carry   206 _____

messages much faster than horses could.   212 _____

Needs Work   1   2   3   4   5   Excellent
Paid attention to punctuation

Needs Work   1   2   3   4   5   Excellent
Sounded good

Total Words Read _____

Total Errors   − _____

Correct WPM _____

from *Buffalo Bill:*
Wild West Showman
by Mary R. Davidson

Second Reading

	Words Read	Miscues

Once a large sum of money was to be sent in the mail [via the | 15 | _____
Pony Express]. The company asked for volunteers. Some robbers | 24 | _____
had already killed one rider they thought had the money. | 34 | _____

Bill Cody offered to take the money through. He was held | 45 | _____
up by one gang. But he escaped on his fast pony. Later, two men | 59 | _____
stopped him with six-shooters. | 63 | _____

"We know you, Bill," one of them said. "We know you've got | 75 | _____
the money. Hand over that pouch." | 81 | _____

Bill had two pouches with him. He had filled one pouch with | 93 | _____
waste paper. He threw this pouch hard at one of the men and shot | 107 | _____
him in the arm. Then he ran his horse into the second robber. | 120 | _____

Before the first man could shoot, Bill was well on his way. | 132 | _____
He carried the money through to his station. He rode over three | 144 | _____
hundred miles without stopping to rest. | 150 | _____

The work was hard, too hard for a fifteen-year-old. Night | 160 | _____
after night, Bill fell into bed, too tired to take off his clothes. | 173 | _____

The Pony Express was very famous. But it lasted only a few | 185 | _____
months. Soon there was no need for it. Telegraph poles were | 196 | _____
springing up all through the West. Telegraph wires could carry | 206 | _____
messages much faster than horses could. | 212 | _____

Needs Work   1   2   3   4   5   Excellent
Paid attention to punctuation

Needs Work   1   2   3   4   5   Excellent
Sounded good

Total Words Read _____

Total Errors − _____

Correct WPM _____

49 The Real Jesse James

Nonfiction

First Reading

	Words Read	Miscues

Some say that Jesse James was a kind of modern-day Robin   11   _____
Hood. They say he stole from the rich and gave to the poor. There   25   _____
are songs, books, and movies that tell of his heroic nature. But   37   _____
Jesse James was no hero. He was a thief and a killer.   49   _____

Jesse Woodson James was born in Missouri in 1847. At the   60   _____
age of fifteen, he went to war. He fought on the side of the South   75   _____
in the Civil War. He was not a regular soldier, however. No, Jesse   88   _____
belonged to a gang of raiders led by the cruel William Quantrill.   100   _____
They attacked and burned the homes of people who sided with   111   _____
the North. When the Civil War ended in 1865, the raiders broke   123   _____
up. Jesse and his older brother Frank went back to their farms.   135   _____

No one knows why Jesse and Frank then turned to a life of   148   _____
crime. Maybe, after the thrill of war, farming seemed dull. Jesse   159   _____
later blamed Northerners. He claimed that Northerners had taken   168   _____
over the local banks. He claimed that these "Yankee" bankers   178   _____
refused to give loans to Southern farmers like himself.   187   _____

"We were driven to [a life of crime]," Jesse once said. But most   200   _____
people know that this is not true. Jesse James chose a life of crime.   214   _____
And in the end, he died as he had lived.   224   _____

Needs Work   1   2   3   4   5   Excellent
Paid attention to punctuation

Needs Work   1   2   3   4   5   Excellent
Sounded good

Total Words Read   _____

Total Errors   – _____

Correct WPM   _____

The Real Jesse James

	Words Read	Miscues
Some say that Jesse James was a kind of modern-day Robin	11	_____
Hood. They say he stole from the rich and gave to the poor. There	25	_____
are songs, books, and movies that tell of his heroic nature. But	37	_____
Jesse James was no hero. He was a thief and a killer.	49	_____
Jesse Woodson James was born in Missouri in 1847. At the	60	_____
age of fifteen, he went to war. He fought on the side of the South	75	_____
in the Civil War. He was not a regular soldier, however. No, Jesse	88	_____
belonged to a gang of raiders led by the cruel William Quantrill.	100	_____
They attacked and burned the homes of people who sided with	111	_____
the North. When the Civil War ended in 1865, the raiders broke	123	_____
up. Jesse and his older brother Frank went back to their farms.	135	_____
No one knows why Jesse and Frank then turned to a life of	148	_____
crime. Maybe, after the thrill of war, farming seemed dull. Jesse	159	_____
later blamed Northerners. He claimed that Northerners had taken	168	_____
over the local banks. He claimed that these "Yankee" bankers	178	_____
refused to give loans to Southern farmers like himself.	187	_____
"We were driven to [a life of crime]," Jesse once said. But most	200	_____
people know that this is not true. Jesse James chose a life of crime.	214	_____
And in the end, he died as he had lived.	224	_____

Needs Work   1   2   3   4   5   Excellent
            Paid attention to punctuation

Needs Work   1   2   3   4   5   Excellent
                Sounded good

Total Words Read _____

Total Errors − _____

Correct WPM _____

50
Nonfiction

from *Ezra Jack Keats*
by Dean Engel and Florence B. Freedman

First Reading

	Words Read	Miscues

Ezra never got to graduation. Just two days before the ceremony, **11** _____

there was a knock at the door. A man's voice said: "Hello, Mrs. **24** _____

Katz. Is your son home? I have some burlap for him. He'd better **37** _____

come get it quick before somebody else does." **45** _____

It was Abramowitz, the grocer. Ezra stepped out into the **55** _____

hallway as Abramowitz confessed, "I'm not here about burlap. **64** _____

It's about your father. He's at the shoemaker's and he's real sick. **76** _____

I don't want to scare your Ma." **83** _____

Ezra had a terrible feeling in his stomach. "Is he dead?" he asked. **96** _____

"Yes," Abramowitz said. "Your Pa's dead." **102** _____

There was a crowd outside the shoemaker's when they arrived. **112** _____

Ezra saw his father's lifeless body inside, draped with his old, **123** _____

worn overcoat. The shoemaker put his hand on Ezra's shoulder. **133** _____

"Sorry, son," he said. "We had to get somebody from the family to **146** _____

identify the body. He must have had a heart attack or something. **158** _____

He stumbled in here and passed out." **165** _____

Ezra couldn't say a word and coughed to hide a sob. **176** _____

A policeman approached him and asked, "Do you know **185** _____

this man?" **187** _____

"Yes, I know him. He's my father," Ezra answered in a **198** _____

choked voice. **200** _____

Needs Work   1 2 3 4 5   Excellent
     Paid attention to punctuation

Needs Work   1 2 3 4 5   Excellent
     Sounded good

Total Words Read _____

Total Errors − _____

Correct WPM _____

from *Ezra Jack Keats*

by Dean Engel and Florence B. Freedman

	Words Read	Miscues
Ezra never got to graduation. Just two days before the ceremony,	11	_____
there was a knock at the door. A man's voice said: "Hello, Mrs.	24	_____
Katz. Is your son home? I have some burlap for him. He'd better	37	_____
come get it quick before somebody else does."	45	_____
It was Abramowitz, the grocer. Ezra stepped out into the	55	_____
hallway as Abramowitz confessed, "I'm not here about burlap.	64	_____
It's about your father. He's at the shoemaker's and he's real sick.	76	_____
I don't want to scare your Ma."	83	_____
Ezra had a terrible feeling in his stomach. "Is he dead?" he asked.	96	_____
"Yes," Abramowitz said. "Your Pa's dead."	102	_____
There was a crowd outside the shoemaker's when they arrived.	112	_____
Ezra saw his father's lifeless body inside, draped with his old,	123	_____
worn overcoat. The shoemaker put his hand on Ezra's shoulder.	133	_____
"Sorry, son," he said. "We had to get somebody from the family to	146	_____
identify the body. He must have had a heart attack or something.	158	_____
He stumbled in here and passed out."	165	_____
Ezra couldn't say a word and coughed to hide a sob.	176	_____
A policeman approached him and asked, "Do you know	185	_____
this man?"	187	_____
"Yes, I know him. He's my father," Ezra answered in a	198	_____
choked voice.	200	_____

Needs Work   1   2   3   4   5   Excellent
Paid attention to punctuation

Needs Work   1   2   3   4   5   Excellent
Sounded good

Total Words Read _____

Total Errors – _____

Correct WPM _____

51 Jacob Lawrence:
Artist and Storyteller

Nonfiction

First Reading

	Words Read	Miscues

In 1917 the first of Rose and Jacob Lawrence's three children | 11 | _____
was born. They named the child Jacob, after his father. The family | 23 | _____
moved often as Jacob's father sought work. The marriage went | 33 | _____
through some hard times. When it ended, it was up to Rose to | 46 | _____
provide for the family. | 50 | _____

Rose had a hard time finding enough work. She decided to | 61 | _____
move to New York. She hoped to find more opportunities there. | 72 | _____
For now, the children would stay behind with friends. Jacob was | 83 | _____
ten when he said good-bye. | 88 | _____

Three years later, Rose sent for the children. She had a small | 100 | _____
place in Harlem. Jacob found the city exciting and a little | 111 | _____
frightening. It was filled with noise, music, lights, and energy. | 121 | _____

Jacob was shy. He wasn't drawn into life at school. Rose worried | 133 | _____
about him. She signed him up for an after-school program at a | 145 | _____
community center. Once there, one of his first questions was | 155 | _____
whether he could use the crayons. Soon he used all the art | 167 | _____
supplies. He loved the strong colors of the tempera paints. His | 178 | _____
teacher—an artist himself—saw Jacob's talent. He helped and | 188 | _____
guided the teen. | 191 | _____

At the center, Jacob first heard about African heroes. This | 201 | _____
stirred his imagination. In time, he would paint what he felt | 212 | _____
and pictured. | 214 | _____

Needs Work   1 2 3 4 5   Excellent
Paid attention to punctuation

Needs Work   1 2 3 4 5   Excellent
Sounded good

Total Words Read _____

Total Errors − _____

Correct WPM _____

Jacob Lawrence:
Artist and Storyteller

	Words Read	Miscues
In 1917 the first of Rose and Jacob Lawrence's three children	11	_____
was born. They named the child Jacob, after his father. The family	23	_____
moved often as Jacob's father sought work. The marriage went	33	_____
through some hard times. When it ended, it was up to Rose to	46	_____
provide for the family.	50	_____
Rose had a hard time finding enough work. She decided to	61	_____
move to New York. She hoped to find more opportunities there.	72	_____
For now, the children would stay behind with friends. Jacob was	83	_____
ten when he said good-bye.	88	_____
Three years later, Rose sent for the children. She had a small	100	_____
place in Harlem. Jacob found the city exciting and a little	111	_____
frightening. It was filled with noise, music, lights, and energy.	121	_____
Jacob was shy. He wasn't drawn into life at school. Rose worried	133	_____
about him. She signed him up for an after-school program at a	145	_____
community center. Once there, one of his first questions was	155	_____
whether he could use the crayons. Soon he used all the art	167	_____
supplies. He loved the strong colors of the tempera paints. His	178	_____
teacher—an artist himself—saw Jacob's talent. He helped and	188	_____
guided the teen.	191	_____
At the center, Jacob first heard about African heroes. This	201	_____
stirred his imagination. In time, he would paint what he felt	212	_____
and pictured.	214	_____

Needs Work   1 2 3 4 5   Excellent
Paid attention to punctuation

Needs Work   1 2 3 4 5   Excellent
Sounded good

Total Words Read _____

Total Errors – _____

Correct WPM _____

52 Bessie Coleman, Pilot

Nonfiction

First Reading

	Words Read	Miscues

In the early days of flight, flying was thought of as a sport. — 13 _____

It was a game for daredevils. One such "daredevil" was Bessie — 24 _____

Coleman. She became the first African American woman pilot. — 33 _____

Coleman was born in Texas in 1892. She was eleven when the — 45 _____

Wright brothers flew the first airplane. As a child, she dreamed of — 57 _____

being a pilot. — 60 _____

When she was nineteen, Coleman moved to Chicago. She — 69 _____

went to beauty school. Then she worked as a manicurist. — 79 _____

Five years passed. In those years, World War I began. Coleman — 90 _____

read in the newspaper of air battles by brave flyers, and her dream — 103 _____

came back to life. She began looking for a flight school that would — 116 _____

teach her—an African American woman. She did not find one in — 128 _____

the United States. But she did find such a school in France. — 140 _____

In 1921 she returned to the United States—as a licensed — 151 _____

pilot. She began performing in air shows. Her act stunned the — 162 _____

crowds. In her plane, she flew loops. She did slow rolls. She — 174 _____

did sharp rolls. She did tailspins. She even flew upside down. — 185 _____

Coleman became a star. She performed all over the country. — 195 _____

She also spoke to African American audiences in schools, — 204 _____

churches, and theaters. "Fly!" she urged them. "Become a part — 214 _____

of this new industry." — 218 _____

Needs Work 1 2 3 4 5 Excellent
Paid attention to punctuation

Needs Work 1 2 3 4 5 Excellent
Sounded good

Total Words Read _____

Total Errors – _____

Correct WPM _____

Bessie Coleman, Pilot

	Words Read	Miscues

In the early days of flight, flying was thought of as a sport. — 13 _____

It was a game for daredevils. One such "daredevil" was Bessie — 24 _____

Coleman. She became the first African American woman pilot. — 33 _____

Coleman was born in Texas in 1892. She was eleven when the — 45 _____

Wright brothers flew the first airplane. As a child, she dreamed of — 57 _____

being a pilot. — 60 _____

When she was nineteen, Coleman moved to Chicago. She — 69 _____

went to beauty school. Then she worked as a manicurist. — 79 _____

Five years passed. In those years, World War I began. Coleman — 90 _____

read in the newspaper of air battles by brave flyers, and her dream — 103 _____

came back to life. She began looking for a flight school that would — 116 _____

teach her—an African American woman. She did not find one in — 128 _____

the United States. But she did find such a school in France. — 140 _____

In 1921 she returned to the United States—as a licensed — 151 _____

pilot. She began performing in air shows. Her act stunned the — 162 _____

crowds. In her plane, she flew loops. She did slow rolls. She — 174 _____

did sharp rolls. She did tailspins. She even flew upside down. — 185 _____

Coleman became a star. She performed all over the country. — 195 _____

She also spoke to African American audiences in schools, — 204 _____

churches, and theaters. "Fly!" she urged them. "Become a part — 214 _____

of this new industry." — 218 _____

Needs Work   1 2 3 4 5   Excellent
     Paid attention to punctuation

Needs Work   1 2 3 4 5   Excellent
     Sounded good

Total Words Read   _____

Total Errors   − _____

Correct WPM   _____

53 from *Sula*

by Lavinia Derwent

Fiction

"Where is he?" The new teacher was speaking to Jinty.	10	_____
"Why is he not here? Is he ill?"	18	_____
"Ill! Oh no!" Imagine Magnus Macduff being *ill!*	26	_____
"Then why isn't he at school?"	32	_____
There was a question! Even Jinty, usually so ready with her	43	_____
tongue, had no answer.	47	_____
The new teacher was frowning at the register. "He seems to	58	_____
have been absent a great deal. Why? Surely someone knows the	69	_____
reason. Where is he?"	73	_____
"Well . . ." began Jinty, and then stopped. He could be anywhere.	83	_____
Up on the crags looking for birds' eggs, maybe. Or away out on	96	_____
the Heathery Hill cutting peat. Or scrabbling about in the rocky	107	_____
pools. Or chasing Gran's cow. Or—goodness knows where.	116	_____
"He's somewhere." That was all Jinty could tell.	124	_____
The teacher tried hard to swallow a feeling of irritation. Then	135	_____
all of a sudden he remembered catching a glimpse the day before	147	_____
of a sun-tanned, bare-footed boy, leaping lightly from rock to	157	_____
rock, coming closer to watch him as he limped off the boat. The	170	_____
boy had given him a bold, almost insolent stare; and he—Andrew	182	_____
Murray—had suddenly felt more conscious of his dragging leg,	192	_____
his thin body, and his pale face.	199	_____

Needs Work   1   2   3   4   5   Excellent
Paid attention to punctuation

Needs Work   1   2   3   4   5   Excellent
Sounded good

Total Words Read _____

Total Errors − _____

Correct WPM _____

from *Sula*

by Lavinia Derwent

	Words Read	Miscues
"Where is he?" The new teacher was speaking to Jinty.	10	_____
"Why is he not here? Is he ill?"	18	_____
"Ill! Oh no!" Imagine Magnus Macduff being *ill!*	26	_____
"Then why isn't he at school?"	32	_____
There was a question! Even Jinty, usually so ready with her	43	_____
tongue, had no answer.	47	_____
The new teacher was frowning at the register. "He seems to	58	_____
have been absent a great deal. Why? Surely someone knows the	69	_____
reason. Where is he?"	73	_____
"Well . . ." began Jinty, and then stopped. He could be anywhere.	83	_____
Up on the crags looking for birds' eggs, maybe. Or away out on	96	_____
the Heathery Hill cutting peat. Or scrabbling about in the rocky	107	_____
pools. Or chasing Gran's cow. Or—goodness knows where.	116	_____
"He's somewhere." That was all Jinty could tell.	124	_____
The teacher tried hard to swallow a feeling of irritation. Then	135	_____
all of a sudden he remembered catching a glimpse the day before	147	_____
of a sun-tanned, bare-footed boy, leaping lightly from rock to	157	_____
rock, coming closer to watch him as he limped off the boat. The	170	_____
boy had given him a bold, almost insolent stare; and he—Andrew	182	_____
Murray—had suddenly felt more conscious of his dragging leg,	192	_____
his thin body, and his pale face.	199	_____

Needs Work   1   2   3   4   5   Excellent
Paid attention to punctuation

Needs Work   1   2   3   4   5   Excellent
Sounded good

Total Words Read   _____

Total Errors   – _____

Correct WPM   _____

54
Fiction

from *The Family Under the Bridge*
by Natalie Savage Carlson

	Words Read	Miscues

As Armand glared at the children, a shaggy dog that should | 11 | _____

have been white came bounding across the quay. It protectively | 21 | _____

jumped between the tramp and the children, barking fiercely at | 31 | _____

Armand. The hobo quickly maneuvered his buggy between | 39 | _____

himself and the dog. | 43 | _____

"If that beast bites me," he cried, "I'll sue you for ten | 55 | _____

thousand francs." | 57 | _____

The girl called the dog to her. "Here, Jojo! Come, Jojo! He | 69 | _____

won't take us away. He's only an old tramp." | 78 | _____

The dog stopped barking and sniffed at the wheels of Armand's | 89 | _____

baby buggy. | 91 | _____

The man was insulted. "I'll have you know that I'm not just | 103 | _____

any old tramp," he said. And he wasn't. "I'm not friendless, and I | 116 | _____

could be a workingman right now if I wanted. But where are your | 129 | _____

parents and who are you hiding from? The police?" | 138 | _____

He studied the children closely. Redheads they were, all of them, | 149 | _____

and their clothes had the mismatched, ill-fitting look of poverty. | 159 | _____

The older girl's eyes burned a deep blue. "Our landlady put | 170 | _____

us out because we don't have enough money to pay for the room | 183 | _____

since papa died," she explained. "So mama brought us here | 193 | _____

because we haven't any home now." | 199 | _____

Needs Work   1   2   3   4   5   Excellent
Paid attention to punctuation

Needs Work   1   2   3   4   5   Excellent
Sounded good

Total Words Read _____

Total Errors − _____

Correct WPM _____

from *The Family Under the Bridge*
by Natalie Savage Carlson

	Words Read	Miscues

As Armand glared at the children, a shaggy dog that should **11** _____
have been white came bounding across the quay. It protectively **21** _____
jumped between the tramp and the children, barking fiercely at **31** _____
Armand. The hobo quickly maneuvered his buggy between **39** _____
himself and the dog. **43** _____

"If that beast bites me," he cried, "I'll sue you for ten **55** _____
thousand francs." **57** _____

The girl called the dog to her. "Here, Jojo! Come, Jojo! He **69** _____
won't take us away. He's only an old tramp." **78** _____

The dog stopped barking and sniffed at the wheels of Armand's **89** _____
baby buggy. **91** _____

The man was insulted. "I'll have you know that I'm not just **103** _____
any old tramp," he said. And he wasn't. "I'm not friendless, and I **116** _____
could be a workingman right now if I wanted. But where are your **129** _____
parents and who are you hiding from? The police?" **138** _____

He studied the children closely. Redheads they were, all of them, **149** _____
and their clothes had the mismatched, ill-fitting look of poverty. **159** _____

The older girl's eyes burned a deep blue. "Our landlady put **170** _____
us out because we don't have enough money to pay for the room **183** _____
since papa died," she explained. "So mama brought us here **193** _____
because we haven't any home now." **199** _____

Needs Work 1 2 3 4 5 Excellent
Paid attention to punctuation

Needs Work 1 2 3 4 5 Excellent
Sounded good

Total Words Read _____

Total Errors − _____

Correct WPM _____

55
Nonfiction

from *The Jack Dempsey Story*
by Gene Schoor, with Henry Gilfond

First Reading

	Words Read	Miscues

The bell sounded, and Jack rushed his opponent. But this time | 11 | _____

he was up against a top-notch veteran. Flynn caught the rush with | 23 | _____

a hard right to young Dempsey's jaw and the kid from Manassa | 35 | _____

went down to the canvas like a ton of bricks. | 45 | _____

    Dempsey shook his head. He was surprised, stunned. He rose | 55 | _____

slowly, tried to cover up. But Flynn knew all the tricks. He pounded | 68 | _____

his young opponent mercilessly and down went Dempsey again. | 77 | _____

Three times the outclassed fighter was dropped to the canvas. The | 88 | _____

fourth time Jim Flynn crushed him to the canvas with a solid | 100 | _____

clout to the jaw, Brother Bernie tossed in the towel and Jack | 112 | _____

Dempsey was knocked out for the first time in his career. | 123 | _____

    "Why did you do it?" he bawled at Bernie, back in the dressing | 136 | _____

room. This was something new for Jack. It was bad enough to be | 149 | _____

beaten, but to be knocked out was a disgrace. "Why did you | 161 | _____

throw in the towel?" | 165 | _____

    Bernie sponged his head patiently. | 170 | _____

    "It was no good, Jack," he said. "He had too much for you, | 183 | _____

Jack. Take it easy. We'll start all over again." | 192 | _____

    "I could have come back. I've done it before," argued Jack, | 203 | _____

almost in tears. "I could have beaten him." | 211 | _____

    Bernie didn't say anything. He knew what it was to suffer | 222 | _____

defeat in the ring. | 226 | _____

Needs Work   1   2   3   4   5   Excellent
Paid attention to punctuation

Needs Work   1   2   3   4   5   Excellent
Sounded good

Total Words Read   _____

Total Errors − _____

Correct WPM   _____

55

from *The Jack Dempsey Story*
by Gene Schoor, with Henry Gilfond

Second Reading

	Words Read	Miscues

The bell sounded, and Jack rushed his opponent. But this time | 11 | _____
he was up against a top-notch veteran. Flynn caught the rush with | 23 | _____
a hard right to young Dempsey's jaw and the kid from Manassa | 35 | _____
went down to the canvas like a ton of bricks. | 45 | _____

Dempsey shook his head. He was surprised, stunned. He rose | 55 | _____
slowly, tried to cover up. But Flynn knew all the tricks. He pounded | 68 | _____
his young opponent mercilessly and down went Dempsey again. | 77 | _____
Three times the outclassed fighter was dropped to the canvas. The | 88 | _____
fourth time Jim Flynn crushed him to the canvas with a solid | 100 | _____
clout to the jaw, Brother Bernie tossed in the towel and Jack | 112 | _____
Dempsey was knocked out for the first time in his career. | 123 | _____

"Why did you do it?" he bawled at Bernie, back in the dressing | 136 | _____
room. This was something new for Jack. It was bad enough to be | 149 | _____
beaten, but to be knocked out was a disgrace. "Why did you | 161 | _____
throw in the towel?" | 165 | _____

Bernie sponged his head patiently. | 170 | _____

"It was no good, Jack," he said. "He had too much for you, | 183 | _____
Jack. Take it easy. We'll start all over again." | 192 | _____

"I could have come back. I've done it before," argued Jack, | 203 | _____
almost in tears. "I could have beaten him." | 211 | _____

Bernie didn't say anything. He knew what it was to suffer | 222 | _____
defeat in the ring. | 226 | _____

Needs Work   1 2 3 4 5   Excellent
Paid attention to punctuation

Needs Work   1 2 3 4 5   Excellent
Sounded good

Total Words Read _____

Total Errors − _____

Correct WPM _____

56 Nonfiction

from Volcano:
The Eruption and Healing of Mount St. Helens
by Patricia Lauber

First Reading

	Words Read	Miscues

The [earth's] crust is a shell of solid rock. We live on the crust, **14** _____

but we do not see much of it. Most of it is covered with soil and **30** _____

oceans. Beneath the crust is a region called the mantle. It is made **43** _____

of rock that is very hot. Rock of the mantle can flow, like thick tar. **58** _____

The crust floats on the mantle. **64** _____

Earth scientists used to think that the crust was all one piece, **76** _____

like the shell of an egg. Now they think it is broken into a number **91** _____

of huge slabs, which they call plates. Each plate is made up of **104** _____

rock of the crust and rock of the upper mantle. **114** _____

The plates are in motion, moving a few inches each year. The **126** _____

movement is something like that of the belt in a checkout counter. **138** _____

The belt rises in one place. It moves along, carrying whatever is **150** _____

on top of it. It turns down in another place. As the plates move, **164** _____

they too carry whatever is on top of them—the ocean floor, **176** _____

islands, and whole continents. **180** _____

There are places where plates pull away from each other. **190** _____

Here molten rock wells up and sometimes volcanoes erupt. **199** _____

Needs Work   1   2   3   4   5   Excellent
Paid attention to punctuation

Needs Work   1   2   3   4   5   Excellent
Sounded good

Total Words Read _____

Total Errors − _____

Correct WPM _____

111

from **Volcano:**
The Eruption and Healing of Mount St. Helens
by Patricia Lauber

	Words Read	Miscues

The [earth's] crust is a shell of solid rock. We live on the crust, **14** _____

but we do not see much of it. Most of it is covered with soil and **30** _____

oceans. Beneath the crust is a region called the mantle. It is made **43** _____

of rock that is very hot. Rock of the mantle can flow, like thick tar. **58** _____

The crust floats on the mantle. **64** _____

Earth scientists used to think that the crust was all one piece, **76** _____

like the shell of an egg. Now they think it is broken into a number **91** _____

of huge slabs, which they call plates. Each plate is made up of **104** _____

rock of the crust and rock of the upper mantle. **114** _____

The plates are in motion, moving a few inches each year. The **126** _____

movement is something like that of the belt in a checkout counter. **138** _____

The belt rises in one place. It moves along, carrying whatever is **150** _____

on top of it. It turns down in another place. As the plates move, **164** _____

they too carry whatever is on top of them—the ocean floor, **176** _____

islands, and whole continents. **180** _____

There are places where plates pull away from each other. **190** _____

Here molten rock wells up and sometimes volcanoes erupt. **199** _____

Needs Work 1 2 3 4 5 Excellent
_____
Paid attention to punctuation

Needs Work 1 2 3 4 5 Excellent
_____
Sounded good

Total Words Read _____

Total Errors − _____

Correct WPM _____

57

Nonfiction

from *John Muir:*
Friend of Nature
by Margaret Goff Clark

First Reading

	Words Read	Miscues

It was a cold February night in 1849. John and David sat — 12 — _____

beside the fire at Grandfather Gilrye's house. Almost every night — 22 — _____

the boys came here to do their homework. Grandfather lived — 32 — _____

across the street from the Muirs. — 38 — _____

All at once the door flew open. Father stood there, his — 49 — _____

eyes shining. — 51 — _____

John almost dropped the little cake he was eating. Father — 61 — _____

never came here. He and grandfather did not like each other. — 72 — _____

"Put away your books and come home!" cried father. — 81 — _____

"Tomorrow we're going to leave for America!" — 88 — _____

John jumped up. "We're going! We're really going!" For a — 98 — _____

long time father had been making plans to go to America to live. — 111 — _____

Now the time had come. — 116 — _____

"Father says he'll buy us a pony when we get there," — 127 — _____

David shouted. — 129 — _____

Grandfather looked sad. — 132 — _____

Tears were in grandmother's eyes. "America is so far away," — 142 — _____

she said. "When will we see you again?" — 150 — _____

"We'll come back to visit," said John. "We'll tell you all about — 162 — _____

the new kinds of birds and flowers that we see." — 172 — _____

"We learned all about America in school," said David. "They — 182 — _____

say there's gold in the ground." — 188 — _____

"Maybe we won't have to go to school anymore," John added. — 199 — _____

Needs Work   1   2   3   4   5   Excellent
Paid attention to punctuation

Needs Work   1   2   3   4   5   Excellent
Sounded good

Total Words Read _____

Total Errors − _____

Correct WPM _____

from *John Muir:*
Friend of Nature
by Margaret Goff Clark

	Words Read	Miscues

It was a cold February night in 1849. John and David sat | 12 | _____

beside the fire at Grandfather Gilryc's house. Almost every night | 22 | _____

the boys came here to do their homework. Grandfather lived | 32 | _____

across the street from the Muirs. | 38 | _____

All at once the door flew open. Father stood there, his | 49 | _____

eyes shining. | 51 | _____

John almost dropped the little cake he was eating. Father | 61 | _____

never came here. He and grandfather did not like each other. | 72 | _____

"Put away your books and come home!" cried father. | 81 | _____

"Tomorrow we're going to leave for America!" | 88 | _____

John jumped up. "We're going! We're really going!" For a | 98 | _____

long time father had been making plans to go to America to live. | 111 | _____

Now the time had come. | 116 | _____

"Father says he'll buy us a pony when we get there," | 127 | _____

David shouted. | 129 | _____

Grandfather looked sad. | 132 | _____

Tears were in grandmother's eyes. "America is so far away," | 142 | _____

she said. "When will we see you again?" | 150 | _____

"We'll come back to visit," said John. "We'll tell you all about | 162 | _____

the new kinds of birds and flowers that we see." | 172 | _____

"We learned all about America in school," said David. "They | 182 | _____

say there's gold in the ground." | 188 | _____

"Maybe we won't have to go to school anymore," John added. | 199 | _____

Needs Work 1 2 3 4 5 **Excellent**
Paid attention to punctuation

Needs Work 1 2 3 4 5 **Excellent**
Sounded good

Total Words Read _____

Total Errors − _____

Correct WPM _____

58
Nonfiction

from *Biography of an American Reindeer*
by Alice L. Hopf

First Reading

	Words Read	Miscues

The caribou came to a blue lake. The leaders walked in and   **12** _____
swam. All the caribou followed. If one animal hesitated, it was   **23** _____
pushed into the water by those from behind.   **31** _____

The little fawn swam strongly beside his mother. The lake   **41** _____
water was cold, but he was used to that. It was a sunny day,   **55** _____
and the water was not rough.   **61** _____

A few days later they came to a wide river. It was not as long   **76** _____
a swim as across the lake, but there was a swift current. The fawn   **90** _____
was separated from his mother. He kept swimming until he   **100** _____
staggered out on the other side. Some of the young fawns were   **112** _____
not so lucky. They were swept downstream and drowned. The   **122** _____
fawn stood on the beach and howled until his mother found him.   **134** _____

The migration went on. It looked like a sea of moving antlers.   **146** _____
If a wolf pulled down a caribou along the edge of the herd, the   **160** _____
other caribou just kept going. They crossed the tundra and the   **171** _____
mountains, the rivers and the lakes. It seemed that nothing could   **182** _____
stop the huge herd as it hurried south.   **190** _____

Then, one day, the herd came to a barrier that was new to   **203** _____
them. The leaders stopped.   **207** _____

Needs Work   1   2   3   4   5   Excellent
Paid attention to punctuation

Needs Work   1   2   3   4   5   Excellent
Sounded good

Total Words Read   _____

Total Errors   −_____

Correct WPM   _____

115

from *Biography of an American Reindeer*

by Alice L. Hopf

	Words Read	Miscues
The caribou came to a blue lake. The leaders walked in and	12	_____
swam. All the caribou followed. If one animal hesitated, it was	23	_____
pushed into the water by those from behind.	31	_____
The little fawn swam strongly beside his mother. The lake	41	_____
water was cold, but he was used to that. It was a sunny day,	55	_____
and the water was not rough.	61	_____
A few days later they came to a wide river. It was not as long	76	_____
a swim as across the lake, but there was a swift current. The fawn	90	_____
was separated from his mother. He kept swimming until he	100	_____
staggered out on the other side. Some of the young fawns were	112	_____
not so lucky. They were swept downstream and drowned. The	122	_____
fawn stood on the beach and howled until his mother found him.	134	_____
The migration went on. It looked like a sea of moving antlers.	146	_____
If a wolf pulled down a caribou along the edge of the herd, the	160	_____
other caribou just kept going. They crossed the tundra and the	171	_____
mountains, the rivers and the lakes. It seemed that nothing could	182	_____
stop the huge herd as it hurried south.	190	_____
Then, one day, the herd came to a barrier that was new to	203	_____
them. The leaders stopped.	207	_____

Needs Work   1   2   3   4   5   Excellent

Paid attention to punctuation

Needs Work   1   2   3   4   5   Excellent

Sounded good

Total Words Read _____

Total Errors − _____

Correct WPM _____

59

Nonfiction

from *George Rogers Clark:*
Frontier Fighter
by Adèle deLeeuw

First Reading

	Words Read	Miscues

—∞∞∞—

[Major] Clark himself led the men swiftly up the high riverbank.   11   _____

Just then, the town dogs began to bark. The men froze in their   24   _____

tracks. At last the dogs stopped, and they moved on. There was   36   _____

no sentry at the gate. Like shadows, Clark's men crept across the   48   _____

fort yard.   50   _____

Voices sounded. Suddenly a dozen British soldiers rushed   58   _____

out into the darkness. Clark's men fell upon them. Clark grabbed   69   _____

a lantern and led the way to the governor's house.   79   _____

Governor Philippe de Rocheblave was sound asleep. Clark   87   _____

shook him awake. De Rocheblave stared up at him under his   98   _____

nightcap. "I am George Rogers Clark," he said. "You have just   109   _____

become a prisoner of the Commonwealth of Virginia."   117   _____

Then the rest of Clark's army ran through the town. They   128   _____

shouted and whooped. The frightened villagers cowered in their   137   _____

homes. "Stay inside until daybreak on pain of death!" they   147   _____

were told.   149   _____

Clark's men patrolled the streets. No one could get away.   159   _____

No messenger could creep out to run for help.   168   _____

Kaskaskia had fallen to the Americans! Not a shot had been   179   _____

fired. Not a drop of blood had been spilled. It was July 4, 1778,   193   _____

just two years after the Declaration of Independence had   202   _____

been signed.   204   _____

Needs Work   1   2   3   4   5   Excellent
Paid attention to punctuation

Needs Work   1   2   3   4   5   Excellent
Sounded good

Total Words Read   _____

Total Errors   − _____

Correct WPM   _____

from *George Rogers Clark:*

Frontier Fighter

by Adèle deLeeuw

Second Reading

	Words Read	Miscues

〜

[Major] Clark himself led the men swiftly up the high riverbank.
Just then, the town dogs began to bark. The men froze in their
tracks. At last the dogs stopped, and they moved on. There was
no sentry at the gate. Like shadows, Clark's men crept across the
fort yard.

Voices sounded. Suddenly a dozen British soldiers rushed
out into the darkness. Clark's men fell upon them. Clark grabbed
a lantern and led the way to the governor's house.

Governor Philippe de Rocheblave was sound asleep. Clark
shook him awake. De Rocheblave stared up at him under his
nightcap. "I am George Rogers Clark," he said. "You have just
become a prisoner of the Commonwealth of Virginia."

Then the rest of Clark's army ran through the town. They
shouted and whooped. The frightened villagers cowered in their
homes. "Stay inside until daybreak on pain of death!" they
were told.

Clark's men patrolled the streets. No one could get away.
No messenger could creep out to run for help.

Kaskaskia had fallen to the Americans! Not a shot had been
fired. Not a drop of blood had been spilled. It was July 4, 1778,
just two years after the Declaration of Independence had
been signed.

Words Read	Miscues
11	_____
24	_____
36	_____
48	_____
50	_____
58	_____
69	_____
79	_____
87	_____
98	_____
109	_____
117	_____
128	_____
137	_____
147	_____
149	_____
159	_____
168	_____
179	_____
193	_____
202	_____
204	_____

Needs Work   1   2   3   4   5   Excellent
Paid attention to punctuation

Needs Work   1   2   3   4   5   Excellent
Sounded good

Total Words Read _____

Total Errors – _____

Correct WPM _____

60 The Lost Colony of Roanoke

Nonfiction

First Reading

	Words Read	Miscues

John White stood on the ship's deck. He peered across the   11   _____

water toward the small island. It had been three long years since   23   _____

he had left. Now, at last, he was coming back.   33   _____

     The captain anchored the ship off the Outer Banks of what is   45   _____

now North Carolina. White watched smoke rise from Roanoke   54   _____

Island. He assumed it came from the settlement where he had left   66   _____

his daughter and more than one hundred other English colonists.   76   _____

Someone must have started a cooking fire.   83   _____

     And so, in August of 1590, White and a few shipmates rowed   95   _____

to the island. When they arrived, they were shocked. The place   106   _____

was deserted. There was not a person in sight. White couldn't   117   _____

believe it. With his own eyes, he had seen smoke from a fire.   130   _____

The colonists had to be here. But there was no sign of them.   143   _____

     Slowly, White faced the truth. His daughter and the other   153   _____

settlers were no longer here. The smoke he had seen from his ship   166   _____

must have come from a lightning fire. It looked as if the colonists   179   _____

had left the settlement some time back.   186   _____

     Over the next thirteen years, five different ships went in search   197   _____

of the "lost colonists." But no one ever found them.   207   _____

Needs Work   1 2 3 4 5   Excellent
Paid attention to punctuation

Needs Work   1 2 3 4 5   Excellent
Sounded good

Total Words Read   _____

Total Errors   − _____

Correct WPM   _____

The Lost Colony of Roanoke

	Words Read	Miscues

John White stood on the ship's deck. He peered across the | 11 | _____
water toward the small island. It had been three long years since | 23 | _____
he had left. Now, at last, he was coming back. | 33 | _____

The captain anchored the ship off the Outer Banks of what is | 45 | _____
now North Carolina. White watched smoke rise from Roanoke | 54 | _____
Island. He assumed it came from the settlement where he had left | 66 | _____
his daughter and more than one hundred other English colonists. | 76 | _____
Someone must have started a cooking fire. | 83 | _____

And so, in August of 1590, White and a few shipmates rowed | 95 | _____
to the island. When they arrived, they were shocked. The place | 106 | _____
was deserted. There was not a person in sight. White couldn't | 117 | _____
believe it. With his own eyes, he had seen smoke from a fire. | 130 | _____
The colonists had to be here. But there was no sign of them. | 143 | _____

Slowly, White faced the truth. His daughter and the other | 153 | _____
settlers were no longer here. The smoke he had seen from his ship | 166 | _____
must have come from a lightning fire. It looked as if the colonists | 179 | _____
had left the settlement some time back. | 186 | _____

Over the next thirteen years, five different ships went in search | 197 | _____
of the "lost colonists." But no one ever found them. | 207 | _____

Needs Work 1 2 3 4 5 Excellent
Paid attention to punctuation

Needs Work 1 2 3 4 5 Excellent
Sounded good

Total Words Read _____

Total Errors − _____

Correct WPM _____

61
Nonfiction

from *It Came from Ohio!:*
My Life as a Writer
by R. L. Stine as told to Joe Arthur

I was born October 8, 1943, in Columbus, Ohio. My parents   11 _____

called me Robert Lawrence Stine (now you know what the R. L.   22 _____

stands for). One of my earliest memories is a scary one. It's   34 _____

about Whitey.   36 _____

Whitey was our dog. In pictures, Whitey looks like he was half   48 _____

husky, half collie, and half elephant. He was so big that when we   61 _____

allowed him in the house, he knocked over vases—and the tables   73 _____

they were on! That's why we kept him in the garage.   84 _____

When I was four, it was my job to let Whitey out of the garage   99 _____

every morning. As soon as I stepped outside, I could hear him   111 _____

scratching at the inside of the garage door.   119 _____

Slowly, I'd push up the heavy door. And Whitey would come   130 _____

charging out at me. His tail would wag furiously and he would   142 _____

bark like crazy. He was so glad to see me!   152 _____

Barking and crying, he would leap on me—and knock me to   164 _____

the driveway. Every morning!   168 _____

"Down, Whitey! Down!" I begged.   173 _____

THUD! I was down on the driveway.   180 _____

THUD! Every morning.   183 _____

Whitey was a good dog. But I think he helped give me my   196 _____

scary view of life. I wonder if I would have become a horror   209 _____

writer if I didn't start every morning when I was four flat on my   223 _____

back on the driveway!   227 _____

Needs Work   1 2 3 4 5   Excellent
        Paid attention to punctuation

Needs Work   1 2 3 4 5   Excellent
        Sounded good

Total Words Read   _____

Total Errors − _____

Correct WPM   _____

from *It Came from Ohio!:*
My Life as a Writer
by R. L. Stine as told to Joe Arthur

	Words Read	Miscues

I was born October 8, 1943, in Columbus, Ohio. My parents   11 _____

called me Robert Lawrence Stine (now you know what the R. L.   22 _____

stands for). One of my earliest memories is a scary one. It's   34 _____

about Whitey.   36 _____

Whitey was our dog. In pictures, Whitey looks like he was half   48 _____

husky, half collie, and half elephant. He was so big that when we   61 _____

allowed him in the house, he knocked over vases—and the tables   73 _____

they were on! That's why we kept him in the garage.   84 _____

When I was four, it was my job to let Whitey out of the garage   99 _____

every morning. As soon as I stepped outside, I could hear him   111 _____

scratching at the inside of the garage door.   119 _____

Slowly, I'd push up the heavy door. And Whitey would come   130 _____

charging out at me. His tail would wag furiously and he would   142 _____

bark like crazy. He was so glad to see me!   152 _____

Barking and crying, he would leap on me—and knock me to   164 _____

the driveway. Every morning!   168 _____

"Down, Whitey! Down!" I begged.   173 _____

THUD! I was down on the driveway.   180 _____

THUD! Every morning.   183 _____

Whitey was a good dog. But I think he helped give me my   196 _____

scary view of life. I wonder if I would have become a horror   209 _____

writer if I didn't start every morning when I was four flat on my   223 _____

back on the driveway!   227 _____

Needs Work   1   2   3   4   5   Excellent
_____
    Paid attention to punctuation

Needs Work   1   2   3   4   5   Excellent
_____
        Sounded good

Total Words Read _____

Total Errors − _____

Correct WPM _____

62

Fiction

from *Abel's Island*

by William Steig

First Reading

	Words Read	Miscues
He was motionless. The cat was motionless. They waited.	9	_____
Then, swipe! She struck him, tossing him into the air with a	21	_____
cuff of her paw. At that, Abel was off and running, the cat after	35	_____
him. Again she snagged him in her teeth and again she let him go.	49	_____
Abel crouched, only his eyes moving. He was bleeding, yet he felt	61	_____
strangely detached now, curious about what the cat, or he himself,	72	_____
would do next.	75	_____
The cat watched. She blinked. Was she bored? Abel felt she	86	_____
was being much too casual about his imminent end, as though it	98	_____
were only one of many she had contrived. He saw a tree a short	112	_____
way off and scampered wildly toward it. The cat allowed him a	124	_____
head start, perhaps to add interest to the chase. Abel fled up the	137	_____
tree in sudden streaks, going this way, that, under and over	148	_____
branches, around the trunk. The cat stayed close, but slipped	158	_____
once, while Abel kept going.	163	_____
He made his wild way to the very top, to the slenderest branch	176	_____
that would support his weight. The cat couldn't follow that far.	187	_____
They rested. They could see each other clearly in the moon's	198	_____
mellow light.	200	_____

Needs Work   1   2   3   4   5   Excellent
Paid attention to punctuation

Needs Work   1   2   3   4   5   Excellent
Sounded good

Total Words Read _____

Total Errors − _____

Correct WPM _____

from *Abel's Island*

by William Steig

	Words Read	Miscues
He was motionless. The cat was motionless. They waited.	9	_____
Then, swipe! She struck him, tossing him into the air with a	21	_____
cuff of her paw. At that, Abel was off and running, the cat after	35	_____
him. Again she snagged him in her teeth and again she let him go.	49	_____
Abel crouched, only his eyes moving. He was bleeding, yet he felt	61	_____
strangely detached now, curious about what the cat, or he himself,	72	_____
would do next.	75	_____
The cat watched. She blinked. Was she bored? Abel felt she	86	_____
was being much too casual about his imminent end, as though it	98	_____
were only one of many she had contrived. He saw a tree a short	112	_____
way off and scampered wildly toward it. The cat allowed him a	124	_____
head start, perhaps to add interest to the chase. Abel fled up the	137	_____
tree in sudden streaks, going this way, that, under and over	148	_____
branches, around the trunk. The cat stayed close, but slipped	158	_____
once, while Abel kept going.	163	_____
He made his wild way to the very top, to the slenderest branch	176	_____
that would support his weight. The cat couldn't follow that far.	187	_____
They rested. They could see each other clearly in the moon's	198	_____
mellow light.	200	_____

Needs Work   1   2   3   4   5   Excellent
Paid attention to punctuation

Needs Work   1   2   3   4   5   Excellent
Sounded good

Total Words Read _____

Total Errors – _____

Correct WPM _____

63
Nonfiction

from *Elizabeth Blackwell:*
Pioneer Woman Doctor
by Jean Lee Latham

	Words Read	Miscues

One day she visited a friend of her mother. The woman was | 12 | _____

dying. She said, "Elizabeth, why don't you become a doctor? The | 23 | _____

first woman doctor in America! You have health and brains. . . . | 33 | _____

"If I could have had a woman doctor, she would have | 44 | _____

understood me better." | 47 | _____

For days Elizabeth thought about it. She was already 24. | 57 | _____

How long would it take to become a doctor? Where could she | 69 | _____

go to study? | 72 | _____

She talked to their doctor. He was shocked. Impossible! No | 82 | _____

medical school would admit a woman! She talked to her friends. | 93 | _____

Most of them were horrified. | 98 | _____

But one told her about the Reverend John Dickson in Asheville, | 109 | _____

North Carolina. He needed a teacher in his private school. Before | 120 | _____

he became a minister, he had been a doctor. He had a fine | 133 | _____

medical library. | 135 | _____

Elizabeth told her family about it. "I feel it's a signpost | 146 | _____

pointing to the way I should go," she said. | 155 | _____

She wrote to John Dickson. Before his answer came, she was | 166 | _____

already planning what she would pack. | 172 | _____

At last his answer did come. He would be delighted to have | 184 | _____

her teach in his school. She could live in his home, read his | 197 | _____

medical books, and save her salary for going to medical college. | 208 | _____

Needs Work   1   2   3   4   5   Excellent
Paid attention to punctuation

Needs Work   1   2   3   4   5   Excellent
Sounded good

Total Words Read   _____

Total Errors   − _____

Correct WPM   _____

from *Elizabeth Blackwell:*
Pioneer Woman Doctor
by Jean Lee Latham

One day she visited a friend of her mother. The woman was | 12 | _____

dying. She said, "Elizabeth, why don't you become a doctor? The | 23 | _____

first woman doctor in America! You have health and brains. . . . | 33 | _____

"If I could have had a woman doctor, she would have | 44 | _____

understood me better." | 47 | _____

For days Elizabeth thought about it. She was already 24. | 57 | _____

How long would it take to become a doctor? Where could she | 69 | _____

go to study? | 72 | _____

She talked to their doctor. He was shocked. Impossible! No | 82 | _____

medical school would admit a woman! She talked to her friends. | 93 | _____

Most of them were horrified. | 98 | _____

But one told her about the Reverend John Dickson in Asheville, | 109 | _____

North Carolina. He needed a teacher in his private school. Before | 120 | _____

he became a minister, he had been a doctor. He had a fine | 133 | _____

medical library. | 135 | _____

Elizabeth told her family about it. "I feel it's a signpost | 146 | _____

pointing to the way I should go," she said. | 155 | _____

She wrote to John Dickson. Before his answer came, she was | 166 | _____

already planning what she would pack. | 172 | _____

At last his answer did come. He would be delighted to have | 184 | _____

her teach in his school. She could live in his home, read his | 197 | _____

medical books, and save her salary for going to medical college. | 208 | _____

Needs Work   1   2   3   4   5   Excellent
Paid attention to punctuation

Needs Work   1   2   3   4   5   Excellent
Sounded good

Total Words Read _____

Total Errors − _____

Correct WPM _____

64

Nonfiction

from *Laska:*
Adventures with a Wolfdog
by Ronald Rood

First Reading

	Words Read	Miscues

∽∽∽

I gave John a call. Did he know anyone who had a half wolf | 14 | _____
we could borrow? | 17 | _____

He promised to see if he could help me. But try as he would, | 31 | _____
he drew a blank. "I telephoned all over," he said, "but no luck. I'd | 45 | _____
almost let you take Wolf, but you'd have to take her puppies, too." | 58 | _____

"She's got puppies?" | 61 | _____

"Sure. Four of the cutest little creatures you ever saw. You | 72 | _____
know their father: Kimmo, my right-wheel dog. Come over and | 82 | _____
see them for yourself." | 86 | _____

This gave us an idea. If we couldn't borrow a half wolf, how | 99 | _____
about a quarter wolf? even if it was only a puppy? | 110 | _____

A few days later I materialized at John's home in Essex Junction. | 122 | _____
We went out to the compound behind his house. A friendly Wolf, | 134 | _____
long tail waving, nuzzled her pups as John reached down to pick | 146 | _____
one up. The pup he chose was fat and wobbly and colored like | 159 | _____
her mother: silver face and chest and paws; black ears lined | 170 | _____
with white; dark fur on the back tinged with the brown of the | 183 | _____
timber wolf. | 185 | _____

He handed me that pup. She wiggled and squirmed and tried | 196 | _____
to bring me into focus with bleary blue eyes. | 205 | _____

Needs Work   1   2   3   4   5   Excellent
Paid attention to punctuation

Needs Work   1   2   3   4   5   Excellent
Sounded good

Total Words Read _____

Total Errors − _____

Correct WPM _____

from *Laska:*
Adventures with a Wolfdog
by Ronald Rood

I gave John a call. Did he know anyone who had a half wolf
we could borrow?

He promised to see if he could help me. But try as he would,
he drew a blank. "I telephoned all over," he said, "but no luck. I'd
almost let you take Wolf, but you'd have to take her puppies, too."

"She's got puppies?"

"Sure. Four of the cutest little creatures you ever saw. You
know their father: Kimmo, my right-wheel dog. Come over and
see them for yourself."

This gave us an idea. If we couldn't borrow a half wolf, how
about a quarter wolf? even if it was only a puppy?

A few days later I materialized at John's home in Essex Junction.
We went out to the compound behind his house. A friendly Wolf,
long tail waving, nuzzled her pups as John reached down to pick
one up. The pup he chose was fat and wobbly and colored like
her mother: silver face and chest and paws; black ears lined
with white; dark fur on the back tinged with the brown of the
timber wolf.

He handed me that pup. She wiggled and squirmed and tried
to bring me into focus with bleary blue eyes.

Words Read	Miscues
14	_____
17	_____
31	_____
45	_____
58	_____
61	_____
72	_____
82	_____
86	_____
99	_____
110	_____
122	_____
134	_____
146	_____
159	_____
170	_____
183	_____
185	_____
196	_____
205	_____

Needs Work   1 2 3 4 5   Excellent
Paid attention to punctuation

Needs Work   1 2 3 4 5   Excellent
Sounded good

Total Words Read _____

Total Errors – _____

Correct WPM _____

65

Nonfiction

from *All Things Wise and Wonderful*

by James Herriot

First Reading

	Words Read	Miscues

〜〜〜

Text	Words Read	Miscues
My strongest memory of Christmas will always be bound up with	11	_____
a certain little cat.	15	_____
I first saw her one autumn day when I [as a veterinarian] was	28	_____
called to see one of Mrs. Ainsworth's dogs, and I looked in some	41	_____
surprise at the furry black creature sitting before the fire.	51	_____
"I didn't know you had a cat," I said.	60	_____
The lady smiled. "We haven't, this is Debbie."	68	_____
"Debbie?"	69	_____
"Yes, at least that's what we call her. She's a stray. Comes here	82	_____
two or three times a week and we give her some food. I don't	96	_____
know where she lives but I believe she spends a lot of her time	110	_____
around one of the farms along the road."	118	_____
"Do you ever get the feeling that she wants to stay with you?"	131	_____
"No." Mrs. Ainsworth shook her head. "She's a timid little thing.	142	_____
Just creeps in, has some food then flits away. There's something so	154	_____
appealing about her but she doesn't seem to want to let me or	167	_____
anybody into her life."	171	_____
I looked again at the little cat. "But she isn't just having	183	_____
food today."	185	_____
"That's right. It's a funny thing but every now and again she	197	_____
slips through here into the lounge and sits by the fire for a few	211	_____
minutes. It's as though she was giving herself a treat."	221	_____

Needs Work   1 2 3 4 5   Excellent
Paid attention to punctuation

Needs Work   1 2 3 4 5   Excellent
Sounded good

Total Words Read _____

Total Errors − _____

Correct WPM _____

from *All Things Wise and Wonderful*

by James Herriot

	Words Read	Miscues

My strongest memory of Christmas will always be bound up with | 11 | _____

a certain little cat. | 15 | _____

    I first saw her one autumn day when I [as a veterinarian] was | 28 | _____

called to see one of Mrs. Ainsworth's dogs, and I looked in some | 41 | _____

surprise at the furry black creature sitting before the fire. | 51 | _____

    "I didn't know you had a cat," I said. | 60 | _____

    The lady smiled. "We haven't, this is Debbie." | 68 | _____

    "Debbie?" | 69 | _____

    "Yes, at least that's what we call her. She's a stray. Comes here | 82 | _____

two or three times a week and we give her some food. I don't | 96 | _____

know where she lives but I believe she spends a lot of her time | 110 | _____

around one of the farms along the road." | 118 | _____

    "Do you ever get the feeling that she wants to stay with you?" | 131 | _____

    "No." Mrs. Ainsworth shook her head. "She's a timid little thing. | 142 | _____

Just creeps in, has some food then flits away. There's something so | 154 | _____

appealing about her but she doesn't seem to want to let me or | 167 | _____

anybody into her life." | 171 | _____

    I looked again at the little cat. "But she isn't just having | 183 | _____

food today." | 185 | _____

    "That's right. It's a funny thing but every now and again she | 197 | _____

slips through here into the lounge and sits by the fire for a few | 211 | _____

minutes. It's as though she was giving herself a treat." | 221 | _____

Needs Work 1 2 3 4 5 Excellent
Paid attention to punctuation

Needs Work 1 2 3 4 5 Excellent
Sounded good

Total Words Read _____

Total Errors − _____

Correct WPM _____

66 **Behind the Lens:**
Nonfiction

Dorothea Lange

	Words Read	Miscues

Dorothea Lange finished high school in 1913 knowing what   9   _____
she hoped to be. She'd never taken a photograph. She'd never held   21   _____
a camera. But she knew that she wanted to be a photographer.   33   _____

Lange worked for a series of photographers. She learned from   43   _____
each one. One key lesson she learned was that a photograph   54   _____
should speak for itself. It should tell its own story.   64   _____

In 1920 Lange opened her own studio. For the next ten years,   76   _____
she took pictures of her rich patrons. (In those days, only the rich   89   _____
could afford to have their pictures taken.) Her skills were good and   101   _____
brought her success. But something still seemed to be missing.   111   _____

Then came the Great Depression. People were thrown out of   121   _____
work. Many lost their homes or their farms. There was little to eat.   134   _____
Lange saw suffering all around her. Soon she closed up her shop.   146   _____
She would take her camera "to the streets," to where the ordinary   158   _____
people lived and worked.   162   _____

Lange photographed the poor. She took photos of their homes   172   _____
and of their work places. She took photos showing the hard life of   185   _____
farm workers. She later said that she took photos of the poor to   198   _____
capture on film "their pride, their strength, [and] their spirit."   208   _____

Needs Work   1   2   3   4   5   Excellent
Paid attention to punctuation

Needs Work   1   2   3   4   5   Excellent
Sounded good

Total Words Read _____

Total Errors   – _____

Correct WPM _____

Behind the Lens:
Dorothea Lange

	Words Read	Miscues

Dorothea Lange finished high school in 1913 knowing what
she hoped to be. She'd never taken a photograph. She'd never held
a camera. But she knew that she wanted to be a photographer.

	9	_____
	21	_____
	33	_____

Lange worked for a series of photographers. She learned from
each one. One key lesson she learned was that a photograph
should speak for itself. It should tell its own story.

	43	_____
	54	_____
	64	_____

In 1920 Lange opened her own studio. For the next ten years,
she took pictures of her rich patrons. (In those days, only the rich
could afford to have their pictures taken.) Her skills were good and
brought her success. But something still seemed to be missing.

	76	_____
	89	_____
	101	_____
	111	_____

Then came the Great Depression. People were thrown out of
work. Many lost their homes or their farms. There was little to eat.
Lange saw suffering all around her. Soon she closed up her shop.
She would take her camera "to the streets," to where the ordinary
people lived and worked.

	121	_____
	134	_____
	146	_____
	158	_____
	162	_____

Lange photographed the poor. She took photos of their homes
and of their work places. She took photos showing the hard life of
farm workers. She later said that she took photos of the poor to
capture on film "their pride, their strength, [and] their spirit."

	172	_____
	185	_____
	198	_____
	208	_____

Needs Work   1   2   3   4   5   Excellent
Paid attention to punctuation

Needs Work   1   2   3   4   5   Excellent
Sounded good

Total Words Read _____

Total Errors − _____

Correct WPM _____

67

Fiction

from *The Mystery of Sadler Marsh*
by Kim D. Pritts

First Reading

	Words Read	Miscues

Matt and his dad walked around the marsh for quite a
while, but they didn't see any animals. Even the frogs and
tadpoles had disappeared.

Matt looked up at his father. "What happened to all the
animals? It seems as though they have all been scared away."

"Oh, it's probably just the cool weather. I don't know what
could have scared the animals away."

"Dad! Look! Bear tracks!" Matt jumped onto a stump and
pointed at a muddy spot a few feet out in the marsh. There were
faint, circular tracks in the mud, and they followed a winding path
into the water on the far side.

Mr. Sadler rushed over to Matt and stared for a moment at
the footprints. "Those are strange tracks." There was a bit of
concern in his voice. "I'll take a look."

"I'll come too," volunteered Matt.

"No," said his father quickly. "You stay right where you are
until I take a look. I'll call you over in a minute."

Matt felt the hair on the back of his neck [go] up as he watched
his father walk cautiously out to the footprints. Mr. Sadler knelt
down and stared at the tracks briefly before running his fingers
across them.

Words Read
11
22
25
36
47
58
64
74
88
100
107
119
130
138
143
154
166
181
192
203
205

Needs Work   1 2 3 4 5   Excellent
Paid attention to punctuation

Needs Work   1 2 3 4 5   Excellent
Sounded good

Total Words Read _____

Total Errors – _____

Correct WPM _____

from *The Mystery of Sadler Marsh*
by Kim D. Pritts

Second Reading

	Words Read	Miscues

Matt and his dad walked around the marsh for quite a   11   _____
while, but they didn't see any animals. Even the frogs and   22   _____
tadpoles had disappeared.   25   _____

Matt looked up at his father. "What happened to all the   36   _____
animals? It seems as though they have all been scared away."   47   _____

"Oh, it's probably just the cool weather. I don't know what   58   _____
could have scared the animals away."   64   _____

"Dad! Look! Bear tracks!" Matt jumped onto a stump and   74   _____
pointed at a muddy spot a few feet out in the marsh. There were   88   _____
faint, circular tracks in the mud, and they followed a winding path   100   _____
into the water on the far side.   107   _____

Mr. Sadler rushed over to Matt and stared for a moment at   119   _____
the footprints. "Those are strange tracks." There was a bit of   130   _____
concern in his voice. "I'll take a look."   138   _____

"I'll come too," volunteered Matt.   143   _____

"No," said his father quickly. "You stay right where you are   154   _____
until I take a look. I'll call you over in a minute."   166   _____

Matt felt the hair on the back of his neck [go] up as he watched   181   _____
his father walk cautiously out to the footprints. Mr. Sadler knelt   192   _____
down and stared at the tracks briefly before running his fingers   203   _____
across them.   205   _____

Needs Work   1 2 3 4 5   Excellent
Paid attention to punctuation

Needs Work   1 2 3 4 5   Excellent
Sounded good

Total Words Read   _____

Total Errors − _____

Correct WPM   _____

134

68

Fiction

from *Beauty*
by Bill Wallace

	Words Read	Miscues

Mama was on the phone when I got to the living room. She   13   _____

had a big smile on her face and was nodding at the receiver.   26   _____

"I'd be happy to," she said. "Starting Wednesday? Eight-thirty?"   35   _____

She nodded again, said thank you, and hung up.   44   _____

"That was Mr. Miller at the Dixie," she told me. Her voice was   57   _____

real excited and bouncy. "He wants me to work full time for the   70   _____

next four weeks while some of the other women are on vacation.   82   _____

And like he mentioned before, he said if I work out okay, it'll be   96   _____

a permanent job."   99   _____

Grampa came through about then. Mama told him, too. Then   109   _____

she asked us if we wanted pizza for lunch.   118   _____

"Not today," Grampa growled. "I need to get out in the pasture   130   _____

and work on that blasted hay baler. Dumb thing's broken down   141   _____

again. Just put mine in the fridge, and I'll eat it when I get back."   156   _____

He went off muttering to himself about the hay baler. Mama   167   _____

got the pizza from the freezer. I got a little package of pepperoni   180   _____

out of the fridge and spread the pieces on before she put the   193   _____

pizza in the oven.   197   _____

Needs Work   1   2   3   4   5   Excellent
Paid attention to punctuation

Needs Work   1   2   3   4   5   Excellent
Sounded good

Total Words Read   _____

Total Errors   − _____

Correct WPM   _____

from **Beauty**

by Bill Wallace

Mama was on the phone when I got to the living room. She | 13 | _____

had a big smile on her face and was nodding at the receiver. | 26 | _____

"I'd be happy to," she said. "Starting Wednesday? Eight-thirty?" | 35 | _____

She nodded again, said thank you, and hung up. | 44 | _____

"That was Mr. Miller at the Dixie," she told me. Her voice was | 57 | _____

real excited and bouncy. "He wants me to work full time for the | 70 | _____

next four weeks while some of the other women are on vacation. | 82 | _____

And like he mentioned before, he said if I work out okay, it'll be | 96 | _____

a permanent job." | 99 | _____

Grampa came through about then. Mama told him, too. Then | 109 | _____

she asked us if we wanted pizza for lunch. | 118 | _____

"Not today," Grampa growled. "I need to get out in the pasture | 130 | _____

and work on that blasted hay baler. Dumb thing's broken down | 141 | _____

again. Just put mine in the fridge, and I'll eat it when I get back." | 156 | _____

He went off muttering to himself about the hay baler. Mama | 167 | _____

got the pizza from the freezer. I got a little package of pepperoni | 180 | _____

out of the fridge and spread the pieces on before she put the | 193 | _____

pizza in the oven. | 197 | _____

Needs Work   1   2   3   4   5   Excellent
— *Paid attention to punctuation* —

Needs Work   1   2   3   4   5   Excellent
— *Sounded good* —

Total Words Read _____

Total Errors − _____

Correct WPM _____

69

Nonfiction

from *Linda Richards:*
First American Trained Nurse
by David R. Collins

First Reading

	Words Read	Miscues

Linda found a room in a small boardinghouse. The owner was   11   _____

a friendly woman named Mrs. Higgens. She invited Linda to have   22   _____

a cup of tea with her, and soon Linda was talking about her plans.   36   _____

Mrs. Higgens looked doubtful.   40   _____

"In England there are programs for training nurses," the   49   _____

landlady said. She sipped her warm tea. "I know of none in our   62   _____

country. Many doctors have boarded in my house, and I have   73   _____

heard their talk. I am quite certain that not one of them would   86   _____

have taken time to train women nurses."   93   _____

"But what of the women who nursed the soldiers on the Civil   105   _____

War battlefields? Women nurses were useful then. Why couldn't   114   _____

they be useful now?"   118   _____

Mrs. Higgens shook her head.   123   _____

"The war is over now. Men believe that women belong in their   135   _____

homes, not in hospitals."   139   _____

Linda refused to accept such an idea. She began looking for   150   _____

a nursing position in Boston's hospitals. Some doctors would not   160   _____

speak with her. Those who did were often rude.   169   _____

"Me? Train a woman as a nurse? Never!" one doctor said.   180   _____

"You have been trained as a teacher," was another doctor's   190   _____

reply. "Go home and teach!"   195   _____

Linda kept looking. She pleaded for any job that would give   206   _____

her hospital training.   209   _____

Needs Work   1   2   3   4   5   Excellent
Paid attention to punctuation

Needs Work   1   2   3   4   5   Excellent
Sounded good

Total Words Read   _____

Total Errors − _____

Correct WPM   _____

from *Linda Richards:*

First American Trained Nurse

by David R. Collins

	Words Read	Miscues
Linda found a room in a small boardinghouse. The owner was	11	_____
a friendly woman named Mrs. Higgens. She invited Linda to have	22	_____
a cup of tea with her, and soon Linda was talking about her plans.	36	_____
Mrs. Higgens looked doubtful.	40	_____
"In England there are programs for training nurses," the	49	_____
landlady said. She sipped her warm tea. "I know of none in our	62	_____
country. Many doctors have boarded in my house, and I have	73	_____
heard their talk. I am quite certain that not one of them would	86	_____
have taken time to train women nurses."	93	_____
"But what of the women who nursed the soldiers on the Civil	105	_____
War battlefields? Women nurses were useful then. Why couldn't	114	_____
they be useful now?"	118	_____
Mrs. Higgens shook her head.	123	_____
"The war is over now. Men believe that women belong in their	135	_____
homes, not in hospitals."	139	_____
Linda refused to accept such an idea. She began looking for	150	_____
a nursing position in Boston's hospitals. Some doctors would not	160	_____
speak with her. Those who did were often rude.	169	_____
"Me? Train a woman as a nurse? Never!" one doctor said.	180	_____
"You have been trained as a teacher," was another doctor's	190	_____
reply. "Go home and teach!"	195	_____
Linda kept looking. She pleaded for any job that would give	206	_____
her hospital training.	209	_____

Needs Work 1 2 3 4 5 Excellent
Paid attention to punctuation

Needs Work 1 2 3 4 5 Excellent
Sounded good

Total Words Read _____

Total Errors − _____

Correct WPM _____

70

Nonfiction

from *Biography of a Bengal Tiger*
by Barbara Steiner

First Reading

	Words Read	Miscues

In June, clouds often drifted across the sky. The air grew heavy | 12 | _____

and the daytime heat was unbearable. Sometimes there were | 21 | _____

showers. One evening when the tigers were eating, the sky grew | 32 | _____

dark. Lightning flashed and thunder boomed. The cubs were | 41 | _____

frightened of the noise. Their mother led them away from their | 52 | _____

half-eaten kill. Just as they reached the shelter of a bamboo thicket, | 64 | _____

rain poured down. The cubs huddled close to their mother. | 74 | _____

This was the beginning of India's rainy season—the time of | 85 | _____

the monsoon. Day after day the rains came. New life sprang up. | 97 | _____

Leaves and grass turned emerald green. Frogs croaked in all the | 108 | _____

ponds. Flies and mosquitoes whirred. Winged termites swarmed | 116 | _____

out from under the earth and flew into the night sky. The grass | 129 | _____

grew higher and vines crept across the forest floor. | 138 | _____

The tigers slept in brushy shelters during the storms. And now | 149 | _____

they hunted day or night. | 154 | _____

Early one morning while their mother hunted, the cubs amused | 164 | _____

themselves by catching frogs and stalking a red jungle fowl. The | 175 | _____

bird cackled as she scratched in the leaves. All three cubs flattened | 187 | _____

their bodies to the ground. Mohta crept closer while his sisters | 198 | _____

watched. Carefully he picked up each paw. | 205 | _____

Needs Work   1   2   3   4   5   Excellent
Paid attention to punctuation

Needs Work   1   2   3   4   5   Excellent
Sounded good

Total Words Read _____

Total Errors − _____

Correct WPM _____

139

from *Biography of a Bengal Tiger*
by Barbara Steiner

	Words Read	Miscues

In June, clouds often drifted across the sky. The air grew heavy   12   _____
and the daytime heat was unbearable. Sometimes there were   21   _____
showers. One evening when the tigers were eating, the sky grew   32   _____
dark. Lightning flashed and thunder boomed. The cubs were   41   _____
frightened of the noise. Their mother led them away from their   52   _____
half-eaten kill. Just as they reached the shelter of a bamboo thicket,   64   _____
rain poured down. The cubs huddled close to their mother.   74   _____

This was the beginning of India's rainy season—the time of   85   _____
the monsoon. Day after day the rains came. New life sprang up.   97   _____
Leaves and grass turned emerald green. Frogs croaked in all the   108   _____
ponds. Flies and mosquitoes whirred. Winged termites swarmed   116   _____
out from under the earth and flew into the night sky. The grass   129   _____
grew higher and vines crept across the forest floor.   138   _____

The tigers slept in brushy shelters during the storms. And now   149   _____
they hunted day or night.   154   _____

Early one morning while their mother hunted, the cubs amused   164   _____
themselves by catching frogs and stalking a red jungle fowl. The   175   _____
bird cackled as she scratched in the leaves. All three cubs flattened   187   _____
their bodies to the ground. Mohta crept closer while his sisters   198   _____
watched. Carefully he picked up each paw.   205   _____

Needs Work   1   2   3   4   5   Excellent
Paid attention to punctuation

Needs Work   1   2   3   4   5   Excellent
Sounded good

Total Words Read   _____

Total Errors   −_____

Correct WPM   _____

71
Nonfiction

from *Dorothea L. Dix:*
Hospital Founder
by Mary Malone

First Reading

	Words Read	Miscues

There was one door the jailer would not open. "That's where   **11** _____

insane people are kept," he said.   **17** _____

"I would like to see them."   **23** _____

"Why, Ma'am, you couldn't stand it!"   **29** _____

"Please open the door," Dorothea [Dix] insisted.   **36** _____

"Well, don't say I didn't warn you," he grumbled. He unlocked   **47** _____

the door.   **49** _____

Dorothea walked into a room that was bitterly cold and damp.   **60** _____

The air was bad. The noise made her want to cover her ears.   **73** _____

Several women in rags huddled together for warmth. A few sobbed   **84** _____

and cried. Dorothea walked around and spoke to them. She held   **95** _____

their cold hands. Her heart was touched by the sad sight.   **106** _____

"These poor creatures will never get well here," she told   **116** _____

the jailer.   **118** _____

He stared at her. "The insane don't get well," he said.   **129** _____

"At least give them a little heat," she continued.   **138** _____

He shook his head. "They don't feel the cold."   **147** _____

Dorothea decided something must be done. She went to the   **157** _____

town council. The men on the council did not want to hear about   **170** _____

the insane people in the jail. . . .   **176** _____

"What shall I do?" she asked [friend and adviser]   **185** _____

Dr. Channing.   **187** _____

"I am sure that [community leaders] Dr. Samuel Howe and   **197** _____

Charles Sumner will help you," he said. "You must go to them."   **209** _____

Needs Work   1   2   3   4   5   Excellent
Paid attention to punctuation

Needs Work   1   2   3   4   5   Excellent
Sounded good

Total Words Read _____

Total Errors − _____

Correct WPM _____

from *Dorothea L. Dix:*
Hospital Founder
by Mary Malone

	Words Read	Miscues

There was one door the jailer would not open. "That's where | 11 | _____ |
insane people are kept," he said. | 17 | _____ |

"I would like to see them." | 23 | _____ |

"Why, Ma'am, you couldn't stand it!" | 29 | _____ |

"Please open the door," Dorothea [Dix] insisted. | 36 | _____ |

"Well, don't say I didn't warn you," he grumbled. He unlocked | 47 | _____ |
the door. | 49 | _____ |

Dorothea walked into a room that was bitterly cold and damp. | 60 | _____ |
The air was bad. The noise made her want to cover her ears. | 73 | _____ |
Several women in rags huddled together for warmth. A few sobbed | 84 | _____ |
and cried. Dorothea walked around and spoke to them. She held | 95 | _____ |
their cold hands. Her heart was touched by the sad sight. | 106 | _____ |

"These poor creatures will never get well here," she told | 116 | _____ |
the jailer. | 118 | _____ |

He stared at her. "The insane don't get well," he said. | 129 | _____ |

"At least give them a little heat," she continued. | 138 | _____ |

He shook his head. "They don't feel the cold." | 147 | _____ |

Dorothea decided something must be done. She went to the | 157 | _____ |
town council. The men on the council did not want to hear about | 170 | _____ |
the insane people in the jail. . . . | 176 | _____ |

"What shall I do?" she asked [friend and adviser] | 185 | _____ |
Dr. Channing. | 187 | _____ |

"I am sure that [community leaders] Dr. Samuel Howe and | 197 | _____ |
Charles Sumner will help you," he said. "You must go to them." | 209 | _____ |

Needs Work   1   2   3   4   5   Excellent
Paid attention to punctuation

Needs Work   1   2   3   4   5   Excellent
Sounded good

Total Words Read   _____

Total Errors – _____

Correct WPM   _____

72

Nonfiction

Lorraine Hansberry:
Dreams and Challenges

First Reading

	Words Read	Miscues

⸙⸙⸙

Lorraine Hansberry knew her family was not poor. For one	10	_____
thing, she had nice clothes. Her apartment was well furnished.	20	_____
She was never hungry. This wasn't true for all of her friends.	32	_____
She was a middle-class child.	37	_____
Her family lived on Chicago's South Side. It was the 1930s.	48	_____
In Chicago, it was a time when housing laws kept African	59	_____
Americans from moving into white neighborhoods. The part	67	_____
of the city in which African Americans could rent or buy places	79	_____
to live was small. The people who lived there were mostly poor.	91	_____
Lorraine's father, a lawyer, planned to fight the unfair housing	101	_____
laws. Carl Hansberry bought a house in a white neighborhood.	111	_____
When ordered to leave, he stayed. Then he filed suit against	122	_____
the city.	124	_____
Angry neighbors gathered in front of his new home. One	134	_____
lobbed a huge rock through the window. But the Hansberrys	144	_____
did not move.	147	_____
State courts ruled against the Hansberrys. But they won their	157	_____
case in the Supreme Court.	162	_____
When she grew up, Lorraine Hansberry wrote a play that	172	_____
became quite famous. She drew on her feelings from childhood	182	_____
as her family wanted to move, and then did move, into a white	195	_____
neighborhood. Her play, *A Raisin in the Sun,* won many awards.	206	_____
It was the first play by an African American woman to run	218	_____
on Broadway.	220	_____

Needs Work   1   2   3   4   5   Excellent
Paid attention to punctuation

Needs Work   1   2   3   4   5   Excellent
Sounded good

Total Words Read   _____

Total Errors   – _____

Correct WPM   _____

Lorraine Hansberry:
Dreams and Challenges

	Words Read	Miscues

Lorraine Hansberry knew her family was not poor. For one | 10 | _____
thing, she had nice clothes. Her apartment was well furnished. | 20 | _____
She was never hungry. This wasn't true for all of her friends. | 32 | _____
She was a middle-class child. | 37 | _____

Her family lived on Chicago's South Side. It was the 1930s. | 48 | _____

In Chicago, it was a time when housing laws kept African | 59 | _____
Americans from moving into white neighborhoods. The part | 67 | _____
of the city in which African Americans could rent or buy places | 79 | _____
to live was small. The people who lived there were mostly poor. | 91 | _____

Lorraine's father, a lawyer, planned to fight the unfair housing | 101 | _____
laws. Carl Hansberry bought a house in a white neighborhood. | 111 | _____
When ordered to leave, he stayed. Then he filed suit against | 122 | _____
the city. | 124 | _____

Angry neighbors gathered in front of his new home. One | 134 | _____
lobbed a huge rock through the window. But the Hansberrys | 144 | _____
did not move. | 147 | _____

State courts ruled against the Hansberrys. But they won their | 157 | _____
case in the Supreme Court. | 162 | _____

When she grew up, Lorraine Hansberry wrote a play that | 172 | _____
became quite famous. She drew on her feelings from childhood | 182 | _____
as her family wanted to move, and then did move, into a white | 195 | _____
neighborhood. Her play, *A Raisin in the Sun,* won many awards. | 206 | _____
It was the first play by an African American woman to run | 218 | _____
on Broadway. | 220 | _____

Needs Work 1 2 3 4 5 Excellent
     Paid attention to punctuation

Needs Work 1 2 3 4 5 Excellent
      Sounded good

Total Words Read _____

Total Errors − _____

Correct WPM _____

Progress Graph

1. For the first reading of the selection, put a red dot on the line above the selection number to show your correct words-per-minute rate.

2. For the second reading, put a blue dot on the line above the selection number to show your correct words-per-minute rate.

3. Make a graph to show your progress. Connect the red dots from selection to selection with red lines. Connect the blue dots with blue lines.

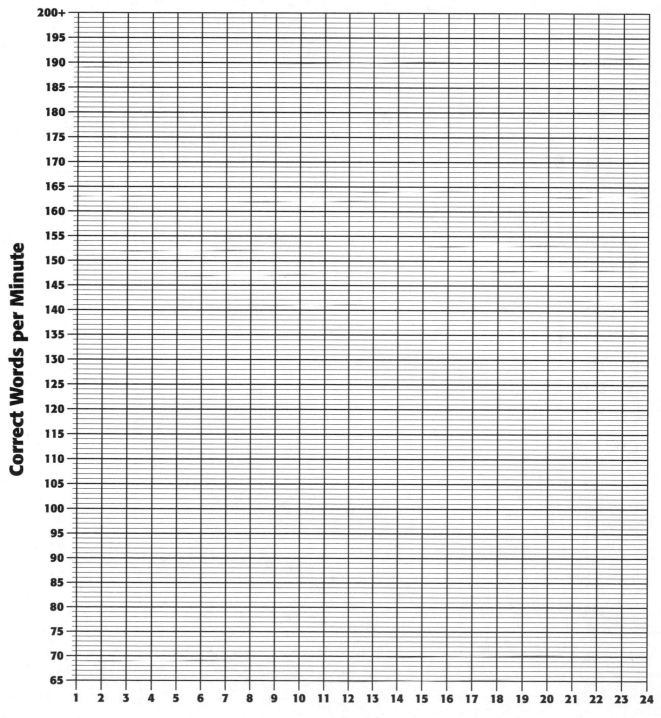

Correct Words per Minute

Selection

Progress Graph

1. For the first reading of the selection, put a red dot on the line above the selection number to show your correct words-per-minute rate.

2. For the second reading, put a blue dot on the line above the selection number to show your correct words-per-minute rate.

3. Make a graph to show your progress. Connect the red dots from selection to selection with red lines. Connect the blue dots with blue lines.

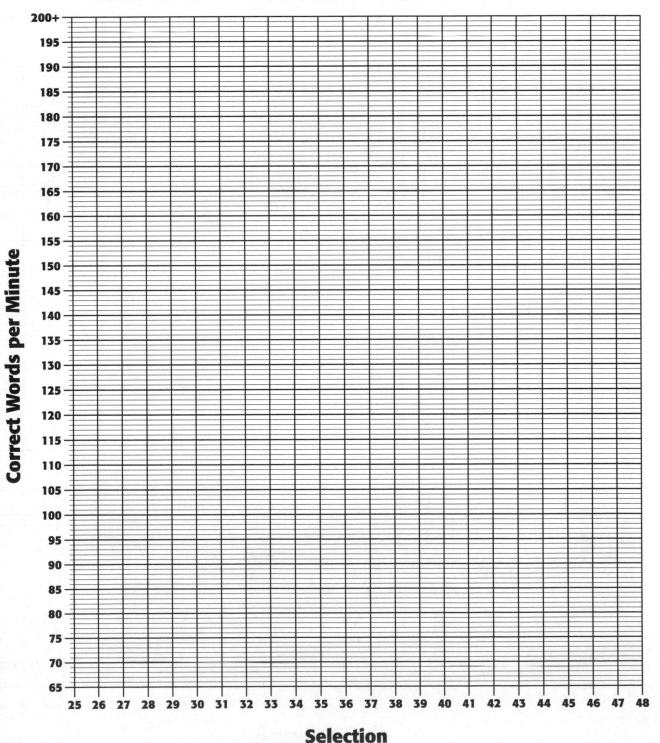

Correct Words per Minute

Selection

Progress Graph

1. For the first reading of the selection, put a red dot on the line above the selection number to show your correct words-per-minute rate.

2. For the second reading, put a blue dot on the line above the selection number to show your correct words-per-minute rate.

3. Make a graph to show your progress. Connect the red dots from selection to selection with red lines. Connect the blue dots with blue lines.

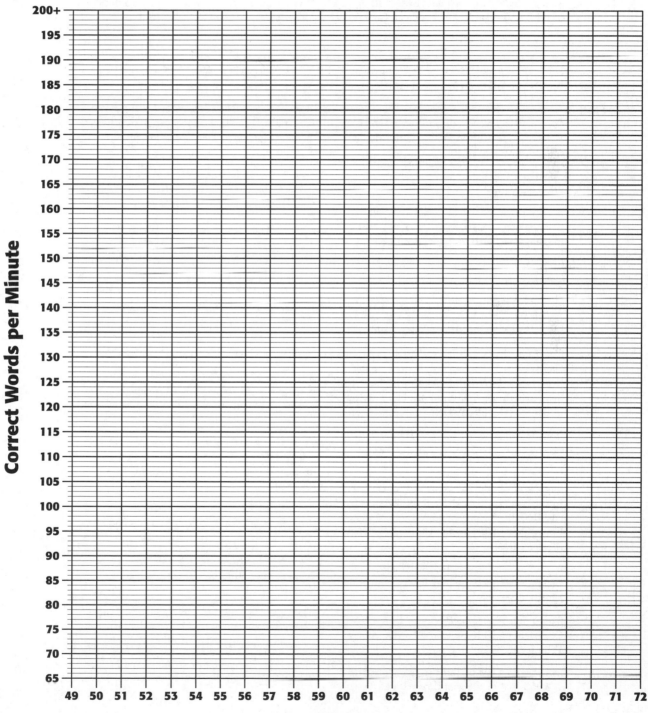

Selection

Acknowledgments

Grateful acknowledgment is given to the authors and publishers listed below for brief passages excerpted from these longer works.

from *Coast to Coast* by Betsy Byars. Copyright © 1992 by Betsy Byars. Delacorte Press, a division of Random House.

from *My Side of the Mountain* by Jean Craighead George. Copyright © 1959 by Jean George. Dutton.

from "The Professor of Smells" from *The Rainbow People* by Laurence Yep. Copyright © 1989 by Laurence Yep. Harper & Row, Publishers.

from *Red Cap* by G. Clifton Wisler. Copyright © 1991 by G. Clifton Wisler. Puffin Books.

from *Santiago's Silver Mine* by Eleanor Clymer. Copyright © 1973 by Eleanor Clymer. Atheneum.

from *Sacagawea: Indian Guide* by Wyatt Blassingame. Copyright © 1965 by Wyatt Blassingame. Garrard Publishing Company.

from *Stars Come Out Within* by Jean Little. Copyright ©1990 by Jean Little. Viking.

from *Adventure in Space: The Flight to Fix the Hubble* by Elaine Scott. Copyright © 1995 by Elaine Scott. Hyperion Books for Children.

from "Your Mind Is a Mirror" by Joan Aiken. In *Short Takes: A Short Story Collection for Young Readers,* ed. Elizabeth Segel. Copyright © 1986 by Elizabeth Segel. Dell Publishing, a division of Bantam Doubleday Dell Publishing Group.

from *To Kill a Mockingbird* by Harper Lee. Copyright © 1960 by Harper Lee. Warner Books.

from "The Circuit" by Francisco Jiménez. In *Cuentos Chicanos: A Short Story Anthology,* eds. Rudolfo A. Anaya and Antonio Márquez. Copyright © 1984 by the University of New Mexico Press.

from *Number the Stars* by Lois Lowry. Copyright © 1989 by Lois Lowry. Houghton Mifflin Company.

from *Addie Across the Prairie* by Laurie Lawlor. Copyright © 1986 by Laurie Lawlor. Albert Whitman & Company.

from *Outlaw Red* by Jim Kjelgaard. Copyright © 1953 by Jim Kjelgaard. Bantam Skylark.

from *Across the Wild River* by Bill Gutman. Copyright © 1993 by Daniel Weiss Associates, Inc. Harper Paperbacks.

from *Biography of a Killer Whale* by Barbara Steiner. Copyright © 1978 by Barbara Steiner. G. P. Putnam's Sons.

from *Biography of a Giraffe* by Alice L. Hopf. Copyright © 1978 by Alice L. Hopf. G. P. Putnam's Sons.

from *Margaret Bourke-White* by Catherine A. Welch. Copyright © 1997 by Catherine A. Welch. Carolrhoda Books.

from *Summer of the Monkeys* by Wilson Rawls. Copyright © 1976 by Woodrow Wilson Rawls. Bantam Doubleday Dell Books for Young Readers.

from *Shane* by Jack Schaefer. Copyright © 1949 by Jack Schaefer, Copyright © 1954 by John McCormack. Houghton Mifflin.

from *Pirate's Promise* by Clyde Robert Bulla. Copyright © 1958 by Clyde Robert Bulla. HarperTrophy, a division of HarperCollins Publishers.

from "Splendor" by Lois Lowry. In *Short Takes: A Short Story Collection for Young Readers,* ed. Elizabeth Segel. Copyright © 1986 by Elizabeth Segel. Dell Publishing, a division of Bantam Doubleday Dell Publishing Group.

from *The House on Mango Street* by Sandra Cisneros. Copyright © 1989 by Sandra Cisneros. Vintage Books, a division of Random House.

from *One-Eyed Cat* by Paula Fox. Copyright © 1984 by Paula Fox. Dell Publishing, a division of Bantam Doubleday Dell Books for Young Readers.

from *Cave Under the City* by Harry Mazer. Copyright © 1986 by Harry Mazer. Thomas Y. Crowell.

from *Summer Hawk* by Deborah Savage. Copyright © 1999 by Deborah Savage. Puffin Books.

from *The Moon of the Bears* by Jean Craighead George. Copyright © 1967, 1993 by Jean Craighead George. HarperCollins Publishers.

from *What's in the Deep?* by Alese and Morton Pechter. Copyright © 1989 by Acropolis Books.